DEATH AT THE HARBOURVIEW CAFE

A TRUE CRIME STORY

DEATH AT THE HARBOURVIEW CAFE

A TRUE CRIME STORY

FRED HUMBER

FLANKER PRESS LIMITED
ST. JOHN'S

Library and Archives Canada Cataloguing in Publication

Humber, Fred, 1945-, author
    Death at the Harbourview Cafe : a true crime story
/ Fred Humber.

Issued in print and electronic formats.
ISBN 978-1-77117-626-2 (paperback).--ISBN 978-1-77117-627-9 (epub).--ISBN 978-1-77117-628-6 (kindle).--ISBN 978-1-77117-629-3 (pdf)

A CIP catalogue record for this book is available from Library and Archives Canada.

© 2017 by Fred Humber

ALL RIGHTS RESERVED. No part of the work covered by the copyright hereon may be reproduced or used in any form or by any means—graphic, electronic or mechanical—without the written permission of the publisher. Any request for photocopying, recording, taping, or information storage and retrieval systems of any part of this book shall be directed to Access Copyright, The Canadian Copyright Licensing Agency, 1 Yonge Street, Suite 800, Toronto, ON M5E 1E5. This applies to classroom use as well.

PRINTED IN CANADA

This paper has been certified to meet the environmental and social standards of the Forest Stewardship Council® (FSC®) and comes from responsibly managed forests, and verified recycled sources.

Cover Design by Graham Blair

Cover photo by Leo Dominic

FLANKER PRESS LTD.
PO BOX 2522, STATION C
ST. JOHN'S, NL
CANADA

TELEPHONE: (709) 739-4377   FAX: (709) 739-4420   TOLL-FREE: 1-866-739-4420
WWW.FLANKERPRESS.COM

9 8 7 6 5 4

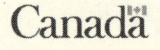

We acknowledge the financial support of the Government of Canada through the Canada Book Fund (CBF) and the Government of Newfoundland and Labrador, Department of Tourism, Culture, Industry and Innovation for our publishing activities. We acknowledge the support of the Canada Council for the Arts, which last year invested $157 million to bring the arts to Canadians throughout the country. Nous remercions le Conseil des arts du Canada de son soutien. L'an dernier, le Conseil a investi 157 millions de dollars pour mettre de l'art dans la vie des Canadiennes et des Canadiens de tout le pays.

To those who died or were wounded in the tragedy, and to Miss Hearsey Canning, who tried so hard to prevent it, I dedicate this long-overdue book.

This true story is from a night of horror and heroism. I lived in Botwood at that time, as did many of the witnesses who came forward to share their memories. Some are now elderly, yet they poured out years of pent-up emotions, many having to pause to compose themselves.

After intense research, I was able to uncover an RCMP file and the findings of a provincial magisterial enquiry, completed in December of 1958 and withheld from publication for nearly sixty years after the event. Its findings and formal statements from those called by the enquiry, most now deceased, combined with current interviews and research, have been used to create *Death at the Harbourview Cafe*.

It is Newfoundland and Labrador's history, within the broader scope of Canadian history, and one of my objectives is to bring understanding to Botwood's youth, who must be puzzled over the various interpretations of this story handed down by elders in the community. It is equally important to give closure to those witnesses and first responders involved in the events of November 6 and 7, 1958. Make no mistake, they were abandoned to their own devices to cope as best they could, with many troubling questions left unanswered. The shame is on those who could have and should have released the report.

The fallout of these events broke the heart of a small seaport town. We never got over it. I was thirteen at the time.

Fred Humber
2017

DEATH AT THE HARBOURVIEW CAFE

A TRUE CRIME STORY

1

Tom Ling, a follower of Confucius, was Botwood's first Chinese immigrant. His true Chinese name was Ping Yew, but he was known to locals as Jim Ling or "Jim the Chinaman." He was born on November 16, 1907, in Tung Shaw, in the District of Hoy Ping in the province of Kwangtung, China. In 1928, his parents chose a wife for him, as was the custom of the day. Her name was Soo Ho Que. She was everything he could have hoped for, and they loved each other dearly. One year after their marriage, a second wonderful thing happened when she brought forth a baby boy. Jim's heart was filled with joy as much as any man's could be. But conditions in his home province were dire. Poverty was everywhere, and even starvation at times because of famine. It was so severe that he and Soo Ho Que held discussions with their parents and families, the end result of which was a life-changing decision affecting them all. They would pool their resources to fund Jim's passage to North America. In time, they hoped, she and their son would leave to join him, and together they

Jim Ling, very young. Courtesy of Botwood Heritage Society.

would provide a Confucius-based family life, one which the Chinese knew well and valued above all else.

At that time, racist legislation existed throughout all of North America, barring females from entry and imposing a punishing head tax on all Chinese immigrants. It was the equivalent of three years' income in today's dollars. The decision to leave was fraught with uncertainty and considerable financial commitment, leaving those remaining behind practically penniless. Once Jim became settled, he agreed he would send both families financial help and would return to visit them from time to time. Further, they hoped and dreamed that the restrictions would in time be lifted, and his wife and child would join him in the new land of opportunity that the Chinese referred to as "Gold Mountain."

Friends forever: Left to Right Jim Ling; Ron Budgell; Frank Adams; Bob Woolridge; Linda Woolridge. Courtesy of Pattie Budgell and Sylvia Brent Rice.

In May 1931, bearing a Chinese immigration certificate, Jim began his sojourn to a foreign country. His final destination was the Dominion of Newfoundland, on Canada's east coast, two months' travel away, a place where the language and ways were unknown to him. He had received information from Chinese citizens from his region of China, who knew residents in St. John's who were operating restaurants and laundries, that a seaport in the central part of the island, Botwood, was thriving and presented a good opportunity for business ventures to be set up, without causing friction with the Caucasian community. Additionally, having a relationship with the Chinese community in the capital city from his own "region" was a source of comfort. He knew he would not be totally alone should he need to reach out. This point was instrumental in Jim's choice of destination, the fact that he was an immigrant from what was dubbed the "region" group. Individuals from a particular part of China with its own customs and ways could bring about unique challenges, often giving rise to loneliness when in the midst of folks from other regions, or from "chain" immigrants. Chain immigrants were based purely on family, brothers and cousins and uncles, congregating in specific communities, wherein loneliness was not so much of an issue. At least they had one another.

Perhaps it is not so strange, then, that psychologist Frieda Fromm Reichmann writes, "Loneliness is such a frightening experience, people will do practically anything to avoid it."

A life of grieving for his wife and son commenced as the steamer slipped out of the harbour in Tung Shaw. When the dock on which his loved one, Soo Ho, stood holding their two-year-old-son finally disappeared into the fog, a wave of emotion swept over him. He found a place near the engine room and wept privately in great sorrow for those being left behind, his heart riven. Jim Ling's future was going to be challenging.

Upon arriving in Vancouver, he went through Customs and Immigration and was escorted under guard directly to the train station, as if he were a criminal. This treatment of immigrants applied only to the Chinese. If he wished to depart the train at any of the station stops to look around, he was required to seek permission and be accompanied by a guard. From Halifax he travelled by ferry to Port aux Basques, arriving on the American holiday July 4, 1931, and from there he soon arrived in Botwood, where he would begin to build a future for himself and his family.

Immediately upon his arrival, Jim Ling bought a small dry goods store on Water Street adjacent to Burt's Lane, from local resident Fred Waterman. This failed, and he then partnered with an enterprising local man named Phineas Boone. They renovated that same building, extending it out to the edge of the pavement, and then went upward, turning it into a two-storey structure, with living quarters upstairs, while the lower level was converted into a second-hand clothing store.

These new partners were hopeful, but the venture did not flourish, mainly because people were so poor in those times they would mend their own clothes, or seek out a seamstress who could repair their existing garments. While people were employed, wages were low and disposable income was meagre.

But Jim was not easily defeated. Focusing on the task of eventually reuniting with his wife and son, he pressed on and over time made further renovations to the structure. Soon he formed a brief business arrangement with Harvey Fong, who in 1940 had moved to Botwood from St. John's. With Harvey as a silent partner, Jim began operating a café. Harvey was not happy in the partnership. He found Jim difficult to get along with, a personality in conflict with his own, and soon they were each doing their own thing. To Jim's delight, after a few years this latest venture became a success, beyond his wildest dreams. He named it the Harbourview Cafe. It would be his very own Gold Mountain, his personal Promised Land. The clothing business continued as an aside to the café. He worked hard, and, as agreed, he sent money home. He was unable to afford to return to visit because of the enormous expense involved. The head tax alone had taken three years' income, not to mention the costs incurred in setting up his various ventures. He wrote to Soo Ho weekly, sending her money and telling her of the progress he was making, and of his longing for her and their son and his hope to soon be able to visit them. This went on for years, this living in hope. It was torture and weighed heavily on his mind, giving rise to mood swings and occasional short-tempered outbursts.

Then, disaster. Out of the blue, Jim's hope that his family would eventually join him were dashed. His wife became ill and died in 1940, nine years after his departure. He sank into a very dark depression, so pronounced it immobilized him, forcing him to close his business for several days, and he spoke to no one. He was inconsolable and only resurfaced after considerable effort by the Chinese community, in particular Harry Chow, and Jim's many new Caucasian friends.

Immigration rules had remained brutally restrictive, giving Jim no choice but to leave his son in China to be raised by Soo Ho Que's parents as the communist revolution was evolving. He clung to the hope that one day he would reunite with his son and applied himself to raise the funds to make that happen, all the while corresponding with him through weekly letters. Finally, after a few more years, he had managed to set aside sufficient funds to make a trip to China to visit his son and family and friends.

The process to do so was arduous in planning and costly in paperwork. First he applied for a non-immigrant registration certificate, "alien in transit," which was issued by the USA on December 22, 1947, permitting Jim to travel through ports in the States for the forthcoming visit he planned for 1949. He also required a Chinese passport valid from November 3, 1947 to November 2, 1950, which was issued by the Chinese consul general in Toronto. The two-year maximum length of visit was the rule at the time. Overstaying would make returning to Newfoundland impossible, as it was illegal under immigration rules. Further, a certificate drawn in Newfoundland allowing him a visit to China for a maximum of two years was issued November 18, 1948. Now, finally, he was ready and set out for St. John's with the sum of $10,000 in his pocket to give to his son and family members to help them in their struggles. Passage had been arranged on a cargo vessel at minimum cost to him by a local Chinese import-export firm from the same region as Jim. He arrived in St. John's, where for several days he would stay with friends and await his scheduled departure.

A knock came on the door, and a friend entered bearing shocking news. Jim's worst fears were realized. His son, twenty-two, had just been killed by communist Red Brigade rebels in the civil war for refusing to join the revolution. Jim was staggered by this blow. His son was having nothing to do with the revolution, and his convictions had cost him his life. With his St. John's friends supporting him, Jim decided to continue on to China to fulfill his obligations. They accompanied him to the Immigration office the following day. Yet another shock would send Jim reeling. During the process, officials discovered that he had a large sum of money he was taking out of the country. He was unceremoniously informed that this was against the rules, at which time a large portion of the funds were seized and a fine imposed for this unintended transgression.

That was it. It was the breaking point. Jim reached into his pocket and removed a razor-sharp pocket knife and in an instant drew it across his own throat. Blood shot across the room, covering the shocked officials and spattering the desk and paperwork. Jim was on the floor, his life's blood gushing out. Frantic calls for help were raised, and the medical team on site rushed in and barely managed to save his life. Jim was conveyed to the hospital,

Standing tall: Ron Budgell; Jim Ling; Bob Woolridge. Courtesy of Pattie Budgell and Sylvia Brent Rice.

where he remained for weeks in recovery. He never did make the trip and returned to Botwood a broken and shaken man.

This tragedy broke his heart and haunted him the rest of his life. Psychologically he would never fully recover. Melancholia was a frequent visitor. He hated the "goddamn communists" and was convinced they would one day be coming to kill him, too, under a cloak of darkness when he was least suspecting.

Over time, as he began the healing process, he interacted every day with those within his immediate neighbourhood of Burt's Lane and The Range while his heart longed for his son, creating a considerable disturbance in his psyche and a vacant spot in his life. When the young children—the Boones, Nicholses, Budgells, Simons, Arklies, and many others—stopped in, Jim found their visits soothing. The peace, contentment, and

Botwood Stores back in the day. Courtesy of Botwood Heritage Society.

comfort he got by visiting with them on a personal level was a relief to him. And so he invested much time and effort in the relationships between himself and the little ones and their families. In time, both the local children and their parents grew to love Jim. The feeling was mutual.

"Jim was the salt of the earth, the nicest kind of guy," said Des Simon. Other boys shared that opinion.

In the opinion of some, Jim was a lovely but very lonely man. The young children were regularly called over to the café, where Jim passed out treats of bars, toffee, ice cream, candy, and potato chips. On Christmas Eve, he would have all the little ones come to the café and pass out more to them all. He would walk up Burt's Lane, knocking on each door, and pass in chocolates to each of the mothers. They just loved that man.

Some boys admitted that Jim was the best thing that happened to them in their childhood. Other, elder residents in the neighbourhood used the word "beloved" to describe the man who made the children feel visible while others were so caught up in their own busy worlds they forgot to notice the kids.

Bobby Woolridge contracted tuberculosis and had to be sent to the Corner Brook sanitarium for a long time to recover. It was a scary time for his family and the community, as the disease often resulted in death. One day he received a box filled to the top with treats of all kinds, with a note urging him to get well and return home soon, as Jim missed him. He was forever touched by the kindness displayed by his friend from China.

If the store was closed and one of the church ladies was collecting, he was always sure to open the door and make a donation.

Fred Gill, a friend to Jim, was a water nipper on the ships. Each ship had three holds, and each required thirteen men to work it efficiently. His job was to provide treats like bars, cookies, cakes, and sandwiches in addition to drinks to sustain them during their shift. These he would obtain from various stores around the waterfront, including the Harbourview Cafe, and it was through this a relationship was developed. Jim would even buy ducks to serve in the café from Fred's dad, who was a small-time poultry farmer.

Fred was fascinated by the Chinese culture and expressed an interest in learning the language. He also liked to talk politics, and Jim was so impressed with the respect being displayed for his country and for himself that he took it upon himself to instruct Fred in the language and found him quick to learn. Unfortunately, Fred's job required him to take a transfer out of the province, thus ending the tutoring sessions, but nonetheless, it stands up as a special memory of time well spent with his very intelligent friend.

Jim Ling's sense of humour surfaced in fine form on occasion. His neighbour and friend James Gill was at the café one afternoon proudly telling him that tonight was his wedding anniversary. Upon hearing this news, Jim started to chuckle. "Let's play little trick on Duff [Gill's wife]. Me go dress up and run over to your door and knock. When she come to door I pass her flowers and say 'Let's go, Duff.'" Well, he got all dressed up and went over and knocked on the door. Duff cracked up in the doorway. "Oh, I must be wrong Jim," he said and gave her a wide grin. That simple act was the source of gales of laughter for everyone for many anniversaries to come.

Jim was an easy target because he had a short fuse, and some teenagers from the general area would tease, annoy, and harass him. This lack of respect would upset him, causing him to go berserk and sometimes forcing him to call on the RCMP. This was how he got to know and befriend a red-haired Mountie, Constable Amadee Bowen, known affectionately as "Red." These delinquents would throw stones and dogberries down the air vent which led to the hot fat, spoiling the contents being cooked and splattering the stove and floor with hot oil. A rather unkind thing to do to anyone. Jim was respectful to others. Why would he not get the same in return? It troubled him a lot.

Respect meant so much to the Chinese, and when he didn't get it, he didn't mind letting the offender know. This behaviour, had it been known by the parents, would have been dealt with quickly and in no uncertain terms.

He was a nervous soul, whom local Chinese elders and locals alike agreed "was a man with many troubles." While offering him opportunities which brought him considerable success, his new life still remained sporadically saddled with periods of sorrow, depression, and frustration. It was a great struggle to fulfill his personal aspirations and meet the ongoing obligations to those family members still back in China. His friends had a lot of compassion for Jim but could never quite comprehend what was going on in his head. How could they, especially since their friend refused to discuss much about what had happened? It was a perplexing, ongoing issue and painful to watch.

Downtown Botwood, 1964. Author photo

2

In spite of it all, Jim Ling eventually reached a level of accomplishment he hadn't thought possible. He was ecstatic when on February 12, 1952, he was the reason for whom a ceremony took place in the Botwood public building, the one housing the RCMP and the post office. He was about to be sworn in as a citizen of Canada.

There he was, surrounded by his many friends from within the Chinese community and those local non-Chinese citizens whom he had gotten to know since his arrival in Botwood. They were all there: the Fongs, the Wongs, the Yeungs, the Changs, Hues, and most of the people from the local Caucasian business community. Moreover, there were his many friends and neighbours who all turned out to pay their respects. His cup runneth over.

Bursting with pride, Jim watched them milling about. The place was blocked. The congratulatory hugs, handshakes, and back-slapping made him dizzy. Magistrate B. J. Abbott called for order, whereupon he presided over the formalities appropriate for the occasion. At the end, he presented citizenship papers to Jim Ling, who was beaming with pride. It was indeed his moment in the sun.

The respect for which he had longed, and for which he had worked so hard, had arrived. Respect from others was integral to the concept of Chinese self-worth, because it reflected well on one's entire family. Had they lived, they would have been so proud of him. Respect from strangers and friends was one of two elements that were essential to a Chinaman's dignity. Jim was quietly and privately considering plans to fulfill his most important need.

FRED HUMBER

When he first burst onto the scene as a handsome, debonair, twenty-four-year-old weighing 145 pounds, he was a man on a mission, a "wanderer," a "brave explorer," as the Chinese would describe those young men who left for strange lands to better themselves and their families. He liked to dress well, wearing suits of fine quality, a long overcoat, shirt and tie, and a stylish hat covering his pigtail, which he wore in a bun. His shoes were dress shoes, not workboots, and he kept them to a Sunday shine. Smoking his cigar, this five-foot-five-inch businessman turned heads as he did his walkabouts. His demeanour, intellect, and style drew people to him. Dozens of people in Botwood considered themselves privileged to be called his friend. And so it was that he took root in this seaport town where people loved to engage him in conversation. His perspective was referred to as "fresh," a totally different take on any topic one could mention. As the first Chinese immigrant to Botwood, Jim set the standard. The bar was set quite high for those who would come later. He had demonstrated that failure is only failure when you quit. His relentless pursuit of his goals had borne fruit, and because of this the Chinese in various parts of Newfoundland were proud of Jim and held him in high esteem. A number of them saw opportunity awaiting in Botwood.

> Mr. Tom Ling, proprietor of the Harbour View Cafe, was presented with his citizenship paper at a ceremony which took place in the Court House, Botwood, on February 12th, by Magistrate Abbott Mr. Ling was born at Hiping, Kwang Tung in 1907, and came to Newfoundland in 1931 He has been a resident of Botwood for 15 years.

Tom (Jim) Ling's very proud moment in the sun.
Courtesy of the *Advertiser*, Botwood Heritage Society.

12

3

And slowly they came. Botwood's Chinese community began to take shape as other immigrants from China, noting Jim's success, as well as the increasing development of shipping through the port and the population influx brought about by the war, began making their homes in Botwood and surrounding areas. William Fong, who had come to St. John's in 1928, moved to Botwood in the 1940s, married a local girl, and set up a successful magazine and candy store business we called Williams'. In 1940, Charlie Chang and his friend Harvey Fong arrived from St. John's and went into the grocery business. Before Harvey's departure from China, his mother had arranged for a young girl named Winnie to marry him. His mother was ensuring a connection with China that would bring her son back home at some point. For a while he'd had a brief business relationship with Jim Ling.

Harvey was amazed that the people of Botwood welcomed him and other Chinese immigrants with open arms. If they needed something, or had to travel, local people came to help, just as they would if they were living in China. It quickly became clear that this was the place to settle, and Harvey wanted to set down roots as soon as possible. Harvey built a grocery store which he called the Spot Cash, located immediately across from the commencement of the wharf facilities on the upper west side of the paper shed, at a place referred to as "the steel."

The partnership of Fong and Chang was a relationship that would last a lifetime. Both he and Charlie were professional accountants but were prevented from practising their trade due to

FRED HUMBER

legislation in Newfoundland. In spite of this, they both achieved considerable success.

Harvey Fong joined the United Church and took his entire family every Sunday. He soon became a church leader.

He soon developed into a respected community elder to whom any and all could turn when wisdom and sober consideration were required. As October of 1958 passed, events taking shape in November would require his steady leadership.

Fong family of Botwood. L-R front: Gerry; Harvey Jr.; Winnie (mom); Roy; Harvey Sr. (dad). Back: Jean (Fong) Jine; Joan; Pansy; Nancy. Photo courtesy of Nancy Fong.

Friends Victor Wong and Tom Hue came in 1947. Victor established the Victory Restaurant, and he would be joined in 1954 by his wife, Boey Chee, and their daughter May Ling, once legislation permitted females in. Over time the restaurant was known simply as Wongs by the locals, ignoring the sign over the door. It became our "Happy Days" place, and there were lots of Fonzies to go around. As you entered the café, you could insert a penny in the huge machine, weigh yourself, and have your fortune told. A thin dime slid into another machine set off a series of bangs and a clatter and out shot an ice-cold Coca-Cola in a small green transparent bottle. Everywhere there were beautiful girls wearing bandanas and nylon jackets, guys wearing their hair in ducktails weighed down with Brylcreem, and who carried a rat-tail comb sticking out of their jeans. Now, that was cool.

Train caboose by Spot Cash. Alan Thomas photo.

In China, Tom Hue had been raised by his grandmother in a time when civil war was raging. She feared for his life and found herself desperate for options. This amazing woman made the tough decision when he was eleven years old, to place him on a boat headed to St. John's, where he arrived in 1927. He began school right away, and in a number of years he graduated from high school while working part-time at restaurants, and at Fong's Imports and Exports. Tom chose to set up the Northern Arm Stores, on the lower outskirts of Botwood, which he operated until his retirement much later in life. He married a local girl named Enid and eventually had a boy whom they named Tom Harvey, after his friend Harvey Fong, who became the boy's godfather.

Tom Hue's Northern Arm Store did remarkably well, in large part due to his wonderful personality. He knew the people in Northern Arm very well and understood that on occasion some of his customers were going without food or other essentials. He understood hard times and degradation very well, and he oftentimes extended credit which went unpaid because of their dire straits.

Upon Tom's death in 1999, people flocked in to pay their respects. Many brought envelopes containing money, and notes explaining how a debt was incurred some years earlier, and expressing appreciation for his kind heart. They were attempting to make good on the debt to the best of their ability. The affection for him was genuine. People openly testified to the fact that Tom had come to their assistance when their families had gone hungry and there was no money. They had never been in a position to repay, but the small contribution enclosed was to recognize the greatness of the man and an expression of the love they held for him.

The Wongs and the Hues developed a close friendship with Windsor residents Harry Chow and his wife, who operated The

Harry Chow (seated) and son Tom

Globe Restaurant. On Sundays they would visit one another to socialize. The Chinese community loved socializing among themselves, in some ways keeping parts of their lives private to a closed circle and reconnecting to their culture. Then came Mok Yeung and his son Stanley, and others.

The influence of the Chinese in the daily life of Botwood was remarkable and impossible to miss, as it could be seen at every turn. They were all resourceful individuals. They created their own employment and did not displace any locals, dispelling any potential tension arising from competing for work in the community. Instead of taking jobs away from the locals, the Chinese community actually created jobs for them. In fact, they all got along very well. They joked and carried on and were so at ease that they could make up fun names for one another. Gerald Mews grinned at the recollection that he had been labelled "Turnip Head" by Mok's wife, because of his head's unusual shape. He thought that was hilarious and took it all good-naturedly.

The Chinese businesses and personalities blended in well. Some stores became gathering places for young people in the evenings, and on the weekends they provided a lifetime of good memories for the youth of the community. There were jukeboxes, pinball machines, good food, and scores of magazines, to everyone's delight. Many of the Chinese and their families attended churches of various denominations. It was always inspirational to see them all file in, Sunday after Sunday. Some would marry local brides and others would, once legislation permitted, arrange for their Chinese wives to join them, or send for a young woman to marry and start a family.

The Chinese were extremely hard-working and put in unusually long hours, and for many that included the weekends. Their work ethic was a marvel to many of the locals.

And in the thick of it all stood the Harbourview Cafe and its owner, Jim Ling, Jim the Chinaman.

In 1958, Citizen Jim was a far different man from the dapper twenty-four-year-old who had arrived in town in 1931. He was considerably more portly these days, having grown to 180 pounds, and now had a receding hairline, although he still maintained his pigtail and wore it proudly. Seldom was he seen wearing pinstripe suits as he had upon his arrival, and similarly his lovely long overcoats and spiffy hats were only worn occasionally. He could sometimes be seen ambling in Burt's Lane wearing slippers, the backs of which were broken open. Perhaps he suffered from painful gout. He was certainly far less attentive about his personal appearance these days, perhaps a reflection of his tormented mind. He felt secure in that he had become an integral part of the community.

Over the years Jim had been known for bizarre outbursts, including long withdrawals from his business, and temper tan-

L-R: Tom Chow; Yvonne Chow; Ah Yee (wife to Ken Ling). Courtesy of May Soo and her mother, Yvonne Chow. Taken at Taiwan Restaurant, Grand Falls, mid-1960s.

trums. During those periods he elected to speak to no one and kept the place locked, with no one coming or going. On these occasions of morose withdrawal he would simply go to bed, and concerned Chinese and Caucasian citizens would try to persuade him to come out. They were without success, apart from those efforts of the undisputed leader of the Chinese community in central Newfoundland, Harry Chow, who would finally succeed in persuading Jim to reopen.

These behaviour patterns would lodge heavily on Harvey Fong's mind as years passed. Numerous people who liked Jim were in agreement that he was a bundle of bad nerves, very high-strung, and continually worried and on the edge of a breakdown. There was no doubt he seemed to be down in the dumps a lot. Depressed, one might say. They just couldn't figure out why.

New episodes of Jim's odd behavior led many to slowly take a different attitude and see it essentially as "The Boy Who Cried Wolf." "Jim," they reasoned, "would snap out of it soon and return to his normal self. It was nothing to get worked up about," they concluded. They'd seen it all before.

Harry Chow seemed to have the secret to bringing him out of his dark mental space. The Chinese community in central Newfoundland was greatly enriched when in 1938 this very young man, starting out with absolutely nothing, moved to Windsor as a dishwasher at the Globe Restaurant. He eventually bought the business, which he and his wife, Margaret, continued to operate for many years, and later they built the Taiwan Restaurant, which later became owned and operated by his son Tom Yetfoo and his wife, Yvonne. Harry, the "overachiever," earned the respect of Chinese everywhere on the island and was unconditionally recognized as the "go-to" person, an elder whose wisdom and personality held great value. Moreover, he and Jim Ling became the best of friends, a natural fit since both men were driven by ambition and determination. Harry had recognized Jim's propensity to slip into dark moods and did not hesitate to do the right thing to help his good friend whenever an episode came to the fore.

Some said Jim "behaved like something foolish sometimes,"

which put a lot of people off and adversely affected his business. Communication was difficult at the best of times in either language, as in order to understand him he had to be asked to repeat his response numerous times, his voice going up an octave each time in frustration. He became particularly overwrought, with justification, when bothered by juveniles agitating and harassing him.

4

But the years were ticking by, and Jim knew it. Now all alone in the world, he realized that his lifetime dream of a Confucius-based lifestyle was slowly moving out of reach. He was forty-five years old when he became a citizen, and he made a commitment to do something about it. Restrictions to immigration, although they had changed for the better, still held many challenges. Jim decided to bring a young male over from China whom he could bring into his life and into the business. From there he would, as was the Chinese way, choose a wife for him, and soon he would be blessed with grandchildren, as were his many Caucasian friends. Perhaps he would even send for a mail-order bride who would become a stepmother to his son and grandmother to the children. From there everything would fall into place. A warm fire had begun to burn inside him, and he became renewed with anticipation.

Because of impediments to immigration, there evolved two ways of bringing "illegal" immigrants over. One was the "paper son" approach and the other the "adopted son" route. The former involved creating a set of false papers for which a large fee was paid by the sponsor. This debt was paid off after a considerable time spent in employment, for which wages were minimal. This could take years after which, once satisfied, the young person could go his own way. It was a form of human trafficking looking for cheap labour and involved a sophisticated system operating within both countries. Much money changed hands.

The latter approach was the "adopted son" route. This involved falsifying papers as well but was intended to "create family," which held considerable long-term benefits for all concerned and ultimately would bestow the sponsor's achievements upon the immigrant, the new "adopted son." It was tied to the Confucius way of life. This also involved fees needing to be paid off over time, and all of this was well understood by the applicant and hence the complicity of the potential "son." Jim felt this approach was best. After all, he had many friends in China, especially in his home district and province, and so his ultimate goal began to take shape. His own region of China was the place to search for a suitable applicant.

Contact was made through the network, and after months of negotiations, papers were eventually drawn and signed. He was in luck, as someone from his own district and province was located and had expressed an interest. He was approximately the same age as Jim's son when he'd lost his life in 1949. Jim was excited by the prospect, but it would take time for the application to weave its way through the daunting legislation minefield. However, the match had been struck.

On a Sunday morning in June of 1955, Jim sat in his familiar chair gazing out across the water from his eastward-facing perch at the upstairs rear window of his Harbourview Cafe. He was longingly contemplating his future life, one filled with warm thoughts of family, of loving and being loved and having a meaningful place in the world.

The sun was announcing the day with an unfolding fan of pinks and scarlet as it slowly rose over the island the Beothuks had named "All in the Way" and which the locals had dubbed Potato Island because of its shape. What an extraordinary harbour this was, with its deep and long indraft commencing at Exploits Island and running for miles inland until it reached the mouth of the Exploits River.

There was music on the water already this morning, as sounds of loons and the familiar putt-putt-putt from a make-and-break single-piston engine bounced across the water and echoed into the coves along the shore. Cecil Upshall was headed over to Lawrenceton early this morning once again to jig a few cod for a Sunday feed for his family and friends. His boat was the only one on the move yet, but, unlike Jim, he was anything but lonely. Moments like these were what he and most Newfoundlanders lived for and had over the years become embedded in their souls.

When away from the water for any length of time, they grieved as if they had lost a family member. It has been said that you can tell who the Newfoundlanders are in Heaven. They are the ones who want to go home: to the scenery, the swell on the water, the smell of the salt air. Soon others would be joining Cecil, and a chorus of engines would slowly rise and fill the hearts and ears of old-timers, who through age and poor health were now relegated permanently to watch the action from the landwash.

Reports were that the cod were plentiful the past two weeks, as was usually the case in June, when they chased the capelin into the bay, where they commenced their annual spawning "roll" on the beaches around the province's coastline. There they would commence to lay their eggs, die, and so would begin the process of rebirth and restocking the ocean with nourishment for other fish species.

Slowly, Jim put the .22-calibre rifle to his shoulder, slid a shell into the chamber, cocked the gun, and waited. Sure enough, a large white and black gull, a saddleback, floated down and perched on a grump on Dr. Gerald Smith's private wharf just across the road and down over the bank from his café. This nondescript wharf drew the little kids from the immediate area to fish for flatfish, tomcods, smelts, and trout. They would then run up to the café and proudly offer their catch to Jim. As a reward he would give them a treat of taffy or a candy bar, and off they would go, laughing and carrying on. Could life be better than this? No! Oh, how Jim loved those children. They were such an important part of his life.

The unsuspecting gull was about to settle in for a morning snack on a capelin it had just snatched from the water. Jim drew the gun to his cheek, took careful aim—easy, easy—and squeezed the trigger. *Bam!* went the .22, and feathers exploded from the startled creature as it was flung into the water. The hunter was now the meal for the many and varied fish and crustaceans crawling along the bottom. "Excellent shot,"

Harbourview Cafe from Dr. Gerald Smith's wharf.
Courtesy of Botwood Heritage Society.

he said with considerable satisfaction. "Me getting better at this," he chuckled, and wrapped the weapon in a towel and slid it back under the bed. This was one skill he looked forward to teaching his adopted son, Wah Kent Tom, once he arrived from in January. From time to time, during the summer on Sunday mornings, he found that this was a great way to start the day.

The work on the docks always ceased at midnight on Saturday, since Sunday was held in the greatest respect by the citizens, and accordingly, the entire waterfront fell silent. No one worked on Sunday, even out in their own gardens. Businesses were closed, and the familiar church bells would begin to chime around 10:30 a.m., calling their respective flocks to worship. Families would soon file by the café, most of them on foot, yet a few of the more affluent travelled in cars and would pick up their friends along the way.

There were numerous denominations in town, each with its place of worship, with the exception of the Roman Catholics, who were few in number. They often gathered for Mass just behind the café at the home of Jim's friend Sam Simon, in Dominic's, or in the Byrne home on the upper western side of the harbour.

It was just another pleasant Sunday in Botwood.

5

Young Nelson Jewer was a good friend to Jim Ling. Every day when he his shift ended at the Montreal Shipping wharf just across from the café, he swung his swanky blue car into the parking lot and stopped in for a chat.

"How are things today, Jim?" he asked in his familiar greeting.

"Fantastic, Nelson. Come and sit down while I tell you." They took a table near the main counter, and Jim could not contain his joy.

"Me got letter today from Immigration. They approve application for my son, Wah Kent Tom, to enter country. He will come here in January to work with me at café. It make me very happy."

"That's wonderful news, Jim. You have been waiting a long time for this."

"Long time, very long time. When he arrive, I have big plans for him. I select a wife for him and have big wedding, invite friends. You and Doreen must come to big celebration, Nelson."

"I don't understand, Jim. Does he not choose his own wife, like we do? I've never heard of such a thing."

"In China, parents select wife, Nelson. It is the way and has been so for thousands of years. It is part of teachings of Confucius, who lived many years before the birth of Jesus."

"I didn't know that, Jim. Once again, you are teaching me new things."

"Confucius was concerned that Chinese society not fall into disarray and that it be a good place to live. So he devised set of principles by which people should live in harmony. It all based on respect, Nelson. He call it 'filial respect.'"

Jim got them each a cup of tea and returned to continue the conversation. "It is an arrangement where both parent and child benefit. Parents give children love, without conditions, in matters of the emotions and material things and offer them wise counsel."

"That certainly makes a lot of sense to me, Jim."

"Chinese think so, too, for it prepare young people to go out in to the world. This not mean that they leave family, but that they become self-supporting. They still very much a part of family and very much connected in many ways. During that time they show each other very much respect. They never turn away from one another. Then when time pass, Nelson, parents get old and become needy in matters of material and emotional things. This then become time when it is parent's turn to receive help, so that they continue to live in dignity and in decent social status. They not shut out from lives of children. They not feel the pain of loneliness. They know they are loved."

"He must have been one amazing person, Jim, to have thought things through as he did. Many people in the world think in terms of simply taking. It seems Confucius believed that in giving in so many areas to their children, it would in time come back many times over."

"Very good, Nelson Jewer. You are good student. There is much more to tell, but that is enough for today. Come back another time and I will explain the 'filial duties and responsibilities' of a son or daughter. I think you will be impressed. Thanks for coming in. Give my regards to Doreen." And off Nelson went, up to Coronation Street and home just in time for supper, still pondering this latest revelation from Jim.

Shortly after that, having returned to Newfoundland, it was obvious to Fred Gill that Jim, for some reason, was living his life in fear and anxiety, a condition that in fact was obvious to anyone who spent any time around him. There was much going on behind Jim's eyes that he did not know or comprehend. For example, one day in discussing his son, Ken, with whom conflict would become quite apparent, Fred pointed out to Jim that the math did not add up if he in fact was his biological son.

Jim looked up, smiling, and said, "I have many good friends in China," and that was the end of the conversation.

The success of Jim's café came for several reasons. The building was perched on a hill overlooking the Anglo-Newfoundland Development (A.N.D.) Company operations. Just across the road from the café, the pulp and paper firm had a large shipping facility, including wharves and warehouses, and its own railway complex. From there, newsprint made in Grand Falls was shipped to ports all over the world. Newspapers were the lifeblood of communication, and shipping made Botwood an integral part of international commerce.

Additionally, the American Smelting and Mining Company (ASARCO) had flourishing mines in Buchans, in the interior, near Red Indian Lake. The ore was primarily copper, lead, and zinc, which was destined for the resource-starved nations of the world.

They had an agreement with the A.N.D. Company to use its railway to ship ore in special cars to a wharf designated for ASARCO, from which it could load and ship its ore. In turn, the paper company could off-load the minerals it needed shipped in for the milling processes and transport it to Grand Falls to operate its huge machines. It was a mutually beneficial arrangement.

Ships from many nations docked at the wharves or moored offshore to wait their turn to tie up. The crews were generally made up of young men in their teens and early twenties, wide-eyed and enthusiastic, who searched for fun and amusement whenever they were in port. They had money to spend, and Jim's place fit the bill nicely, especially since there were so many opportunities to mingle with the young locals who hung out there.

With years of uncertainty in the fishery, anxious families from tiny nearby communities, called "outports," moved to Botwood, to find employment. Some families from Burnt Arm and Brown's Arm floated their houses across the harbour to relocate them on the shoreline in Botwood.

As the town developed, various businesses sprang up, including wholesale distributors, hotels, jewellery stores, barbershops, grocery and butcher shops, taxi stands and dry goods outlets. These businesses became magnets for travelling salesmen with goods to sell. This often required overnight accommodations, and restaurants. In this way, "Gold Mountain" had come to Jim, and not the other way around, as was the experience of early Chinese immigrants working in the gold rush on the west coast of Canada.

Over time, the café would evolve into a mysterious yet alluring place, the subject of rumours and outrageous speculation. Depending on the time of day, at any one time there were incompatible lifestyles being accommodated in the café. During the day, it was a confectionery store and restaurant and a fast food joint, where children went alone or sometimes with their parents.

The surrounding area of Burt's Lane and Circular Road, popularly known as The Range, and the western side of the café, the Peter's Arm area including Wireless Road, was overrun with kids. They were part of the great wave of children that came out of nowhere at the end of the Second World War. The "boomers" had arrived, and the world was in the middle of a demographic shift. While they had little money to spend, their sheer numbers made business profitable. Jim often would invite them to eat with him in the kitchen, or in the upstairs living quarters. On those occasions he prepared special dishes not offered to the general public, but which were in fact the "real" Chinese food he ate back in China.

Salesmen, and shoppers flowing back and forth from the outlying communities, from Leading Tickles to Fortune Harbour, were excellent sources of revenue as well, and business thrived. Jim could not handle all the work alone and would soon have to hire help for general maintenance, cooking, serving, and cleaning.

6

The day Jim had been longing for and boasting about finally arrived. As expected, twenty-three year-old Wah Kent Tom came on the scene in January 1956. He would be known as Ken Ling in Botwood. It was a defining moment. Life changed immediately for Jim and for the entire neighbourhood, including adults and children alike.

To put it another way, the gate to hell swung open wide that day, and anxiety and outright hatred found its way into their lives. The effect was not gradual at all. It was instantaneous.

To many, Ken was believed to be Jim's biological son because Jim said so, and did so proudly.

Ken was having none of it and rejected that claim right at the outset. He let everyone know that fact in no uncertain terms, a source of considerable embarrassment to Jim. This was meant to be kept confidential between "father and son." Knowledge of this fact could give rise to immigration issues. Moreover, it was a disrespectful thing to do. Jim lost face, something terrible to happen to any Chinese person, for it suggested that Jim was a liar.

Jim didn't say too much regarding that revelation but resolved to let it dissipate with time. But he certainly did not forget the sting of that moment. He worked at embracing Ken into the business, learning what his skill sets were, and finding the most efficient and effective way to work together. No doubt about it, Ken was a tremendous cook, but there were so many other chores to be done. They had no hired help at that time, as so much money was used in purchasing Ken's papers and paying for his transportation to Botwood. Father and son cautiously got to know one another, and little by little Ken became familiar with the neighbourhood parents and children. He worked hard at finding favour with the children by giving away treats free of charge. This caused Jim real concern, especially in light of the fragile financial situation of the café. But in spite of some brief differences of opinion and minor arguments, they seemed to be working reasonably well together.

After a few months, Jim privately broached the subject of marriage with Ken. He thought it was time now to look for a suitable bride for him. "What do you mean?" said Ken. "I am already married. I got married in Hong Kong before I came over."

"What? What? You are already married? No, no! This cannot be. That is not Chinese way. Father to choose wife for son. Father must choose!"

"It is old way. I believe in new way. I love her very much. She is beautiful person. Her name Ah Yee. She wait in Hong Kong until it is time to come to Botwood with baby."

"Baby? Baby? You have baby? This cannot be!"

"Yes, it is true. We got married in 1954 in Hong Kong. We have a beautiful baby son. His name Don Tom."

Jim nearly fell over with the mixed feelings of surprise, disappointment, and, oddly enough, a sense of contained happiness, as images of a daughter-in-law and a grandson flashed across his mind. "This must remain private matter between us, you understand? Do not tell anyone, do you hear? You have turned back on rules of Confucius, rules that guide my life, Ken. You have hurt me deeply. I have much to think about now. We speak to no one about this, no one, not even best friends." This they agreed to do. It would be their secret, in spite of their differences. This was too private and delicate a subject to

Don Tom, son of Ken Ling and Ah Yee. Courtesy of May Soo and Yvonne Chow.

become a topic of general discussion in the community, and so it was not even discussed among Jim's long-time friends in his inner circle.

Jim's fantasies of selecting a wife for his son and living out the ultimate Chinese accomplishment were cut short by these revelations. Ken was a "new age" person who had turned away from the teachings of Confucius, the tried and proven centuries-old ways, and disrespected his father. That was a particularly difficult day.

This shaming and betrayal sent Jim's mind into a dark place and ignited an internal rage that would only escalate over time, manifesting itself in arguments and confrontations, some quite heated. The frequency and intensity of the clashes were things witnesses could not get a handle on since they were in the dark at to the underlying reasons. But there was nothing normal about it. This they all agreed.

Unknown to anyone at the time, something was very much amiss with the Lings. While it was true that Ken's wife was planning to come to Botwood, the constant bickering had taken a toll on Ken. One day, immersed in an episode of melancholia, he decided to write Ah Yee and tell her everything. He left nothing out and perhaps may have embellished the confrontations and hostile environment. In any case, it was enough to turn the tide. Ah Yee told Ken that there was no way was she coming to face a situation like that with Don Tom. Ken was left trying to figure out a way to resolve the situation for all concerned.

In 1953, when Ah Yee and Ken first met, it was love at first sight. While it may have been inappropriate within their customs, this young man and woman felt the chemistry, and come hell or high water, they were going to be married. Ignoring advice to the contrary, they did so in late 1954. Realizing that Ken had already contracted to go to Botwood and that certain obligations surrounded that, financial and work-wise, they were both reconciled to his duties. In time they would be together and live out their dream. Chinese, after all, were no strangers to delayed gratification. It is little wonder that Ken was frustrated, separated from his beautiful wife, and longing to embrace his baby son, Don Tom. He couldn't handle the loneliness. Conflicting worlds were on a collision course. Yet he had obligations to Jim, and as much as he would like to, he just couldn't up and leave and go to Montreal, where he and his wife had connections. It was a matter of honour. Perhaps things would get better here in Botwood. He would try his best to get along with Jim and create a more pleasant atmosphere.

7

Edgar Buckley showed up at the café looking for work. Ken had been working there more than a year now and had embraced the role of cook, at which he excelled. Work was required to keep the café maintained for the health department regulations, plus repairs to windows, all necessary to keep the building weathertight. The health inspector had been applying pressure to bring the café in line with regulations, but there was simply no time, as the Lings were busy enough as it was to attend to such things. The abrasiveness between father and son had not gone unnoticed by anyone since Ken's arrival, including Buckley. Edgar could do odd jobs, including plumbing and carpentry. He was a single man, with a young son living in Bishop's Falls whom he loved and spoke about all the time.

Jim was impressed with his qualities and decided to hire him, much to Edgar's delight. It was a good decision, as he proved to be a great employee, one Jim could trust and rely on. In July of 1958, Edgar was assigned the big job of building an extension on the rear of the building, with space to accommodate wood, and a storage room for soft coal. This task was scheduled for completion in late October. The lower level of the café was heated by a huge wood- and coal-burning potbelly stove placed directly in the centre, while upstairs in the two-bedroom living quarters there was to be a much smaller coal-burning stove, presently disconnected and due to be replaced. Installation was awaiting the completion of the extension. He finished the project just in time, for the nights were coming early now, as winter was slowly closing in.

8

Hearsey Canning was a teenaged girl not much different than a lot of the girls her age. She lived with her mother, Cecelia, alongside her niece Linda and her mother, Ada, down by Wong's Restaurant. Hearsey had heard of the Harbourview Cafe in her early teens from family members and used to visit there occasionally as a customer as far back as 1953, hanging out with the other young people. One day in early July 1957, having finished her shift as a servant girl, she stopped in for a visit while out for a walk. She wasn't happy with her current job because her employer gave her no respect and made her feel small. She couldn't help but notice the pressure Jim and his son Ken were under with a café full of customers. She had observed the two of them for a long time and knew they disagreed a lot. Sometimes it was difficult to watch.

When the customers began to disperse and things had settled down somewhat, Hearsey approached Jim with an offer to help. "I couldn't help but notice how busy you are. Sure, you are run off your feet, b'y. If you need help, I have experience waitressing and doing household chores, and I'm available."

"Come back tomorrow and we talk," said Jim, and she did. The blonde-haired, amiable Hearsey was hired right away on July 8, 1957. She proved to be the most honest, hard-working, and loyal employee any employer could hope for. Jim didn't realize it at the time, but she would prove to be his very best friend, a most respectful person who looked out for his best interests. Their respect for one another grew and solidified over the months.

So great was Jim's respect for Hearsey that at each day's

Hearsey Canning in later years.
Courtesy of Hugo Thulgreen.

end he sat across from her when the money taken in was counted. Hearsey would count out the money while Jim watched. Then, to double-check, Jim would count it out, and Hearsey would write the figures down, indicating the denominations, ensuring accuracy. Then Jim would take a large sum of that money and place it in a bag and pass it to Ken. This was intended for Ken to send to his wife for support. It was a considerable sum, and the procedure was followed daily. Jim knew all about honour and doing the right thing, as after all these years he continued to send money back home to support his extended family. That was the deal. Though he had not met or spoken with Ah Yee, he knew all about obligations. It was how he was raised. Ken had been here now for some considerable time. He had no girlfriends. It must have been a lonely existence, living as they both did, and he remained faithful to her.

9

The café was by no means a five-star establishment. Few could afford upscale meals. Jim was an excellent cook, as was Ken, and the menu was not restricted to fast foods such as hot turkey sandwiches and fish and chips. Jim's real Chinese meals were without equal. When Jim despaired over some unsolvable issue, he cooked high-end, complicated meals for those special friends who had reached out to him with help and advice to console him in his hour of need.

On occasion, Hearsey noticed that a normally docile, friendly, and considerate Jim would be "quick" with some of the patrons, and even some of his friends. She asked about it and was told that many people who work in restaurant kitchens have to concentrate on numerous dishes at the same time, all requiring different ingredients and cooking times and styles.

In a hot kitchen, distractions could easily result in a spoiled dish, and an unhappy client may never come back. This is what would put Jim on edge and caused him to lash out inappropriately. Unfortunately, he became saddled with a reputation for being short-tempered, a disposition far removed from his normal ways. She would learn in time that he was under many pressures that contributed to his bad nerves.

Inspections by the health department were a normal part of being in the restaurant business, and Warrick Swyers, the local inspector, called into the Harbourview Cafe as he did at Wong's, the Poplar Inn, the Web, and the Sea Breeze. Jim's place was no different, but Hearsey, soon after being hired in July 1957, noticed that Jim would pay little or no heed to his instructions, perhaps assuming by doing so the issues would go away. She knew better, but it was his business, after all, not hers. If he neglected the health department, he did so at his peril. Perhaps one day it would come back to haunt him. It disappointed Swyers, a congenial sort of fellow, that Jim had such a total and utter disregard for the rules and saw the inspector as merely an annoyance. Yes, it bothered Jim, but he was so run off his feet, he had more pressing issues to deal with daily.

When evening came and the supper meals concluded, the café morphed into a teenagers' hangout. It was the 1950s, and music was changing the world. With their cutting-edge movies, James Dean, Marlon Brando, Brigitte Bardot, and Marilyn Monroe were influencing the attitudes of young men and women. The "teenager" had evolved, separating childhood from adulthood with new-found freedom and challenges.

A band back in the day. Courtesy of Botwood Heritage Society.

After school and early after supper, they streamed in with their friends, anxious to pump loose change into the jukebox and buy Coca-Cola and chips and burgers.

Rock 'n' roll quickly brushed aside Frankie Lane, Doris Day, and Old Blue Eyes, to replace them with Bobby Darin, Brenda Lee, Connie Francis, Elvis, Johnny Cash, and Roy Orbison. The café was humming. There were none of today's recreational drugs, and very little drinking among teenagers. Officially, Jim served no liquor or beer, since his was an unlicensed establishment. Haig Ale was as close as it came to booze. Its alcohol content was so minimal it was classed as a soft drink and didn't require a liquor licence.

The kids who came to the café cared little about booze. They were dizzy on the atmosphere of fellowship, food, and the intoxicating music. Some stayed late, but usually around 10:30 p.m. they would make their way home. It was a time of freedom, not riches. The kids had little money, but whatever they had went into the new amusements shared with friends. At home, parents fretted about the next dollar. They were laden with chores that were never-ending.

10

Late in the evenings, Jim hosted regular card games for his adult fiends. Among them were Frank Adams, the Nicholses, Boones, Gills, and Balls. While Jim was not a drinker, he certainly knew how to make beer. Unknown to most of these people, Jim was a very lonely man who after all these years still mourned the loss of his loved ones. In a constant state of grief and suffering from many recurring episodes of melancholia, he often felt empty and unfulfilled in the Chinese sense. These nighttime gambling events were merely a smokescreen, his means of coping with sadness. Jim and his friends longed for the evening card games to break up the long, drawn-out winters, and to keep the games friendly, the stakes were small.

Occasionally, Jim would close the café and invite only his Chinese friends from his "region" around the province in to gamble. These gambling marathons lasted days, and the stakes were much higher. These events were unusual in the eyes of the locals, and they could only shake their heads in amazement.

The Harbourview Cafe also developed another business sideline, according to Hugo Thulgreen, also know as Tex Canning. Tex revealed his connection to an illegal and profitable undertaking. Jim's business diversified into a speakeasy. In Botwood, there were only two public places to get an alcoholic drink. The Argyle Hotel had a tavern, where people going to and from work would gather for a few beers. It closed at 11:00 p.m. The other was the Legion Club on Circular Road, which only opened at 6:00 p.m., but it had a strict dress code and was restricted to members only. Guests had to be signed in by a member. It was quite civilized: a jacket-and-tie establishment. This presented a problem for sailors ashore after weeks at sea, men who were loud and who loved bawdy jokes and letting off steam.

Jim offered the perfect solution. His café was right alongside the docks, and it certainly beat drinking aboard ship.

Jim dreamed up a spoken code for his visitors. When his patrons in the know requested a Coke, he would reply, "Do you want a ten-cent Coke or a fifty-cent Coke?"

If one answered with "a ten-cent Coke," then that's what was served. If the answer was "a fifty-cent Coke," the patron would get an ounce of rum topped up with Coke. This arrangement continued uninterrupted. The serious drinkers were extremely grateful for having liquor served late at night.

Jim also had a scheme when it came to beer. "I want a fifty-cent beer" would get the patron a home brew in a Haig Ale bottle, but if a person ordered a twenty-cent beer, he received a regular bottle of Haig Ale. The serving of alcohol without a licence went on all evening, for the most part, unknown to the teenagers who were dancing and enjoying their Cokes and chips. When they did figure it out, they said nothing about it, and the more adventurous would order a fifty-cent, rum-laced Coke or homebrew.

This went on for years, during which time Jim earned considerable money in the liquor business. After all, a twenty-six-ounce bottle of rum cost only $1.80 in those times.

Jim always carried a huge wad of roll-up money on him. He didn't believe in banks, but in the back of the café he had a huge 800-pound safe, which he visited often. Alongside the safe was a twelve-gauge shotgun. This was common knowledge among the inner circle.

Hugo Thulgreen worked in Grand Falls as a wildlife officer, and by chance his office was located next to the liquor store. He had a liquor ration book, a government requirement in those days. Rationing regulated how much you could buy at any one time, or within a month. The liquor regulations were driven by the church and organizations that were concerned and vigilant that the province might become a drunkard's paradise. The rationing remained in force for many years and stands as a remarkable example of the power of the churches to influence government policy.

Jim, being an unlicensed businessman, did not possess a liquor book, so he would ask Tex to pick him up a couple of bottles from time to time, for which he would reimburse him. In addition, he would treat Tex to an outstanding, authentic Chinese meal. Part of the ritual for Tex was a double rum and Coke at no charge. Jim topped off the meal with a slice of his famous coconut cream pie. There were many other people with liquor books who operated in the shadows, and those special friends kept Jim supplied with all the rum he needed.

Jim Ling's safe, found in an abandoned building in Botwood, 2017. Author photo.

11

Ken was a slender young man at five feet three inches and 115 pounds. His hair was jet black, and he prided himself on being presentable. He wore tight-fitting flared pants and high black boots with very long pointed toes. He liked to buff them to a sharp shine. His long leather wallet, attached to a very long brass chain, was always protruding from his right back pants pocket. He drew attention to himself when he went downtown to Frank Adams's store, the post office, or the movies at the Imperial Theatre. While Ah Yee remained in Hong Kong, Ken, understandably, needed to get out of the café and entertained himself that way. Occasionally he even went to the theatre in Grand Falls.

The Imperial Theatre. Courtesy of Botwood Heritage Society.

Ken was an exceptional cook and could do it all, but his specialty was beef jerky, a recipe he had conceived all on his own. He could be hilarious sometimes, especially when working in the kitchen. After Antle's Store had dropped in a side of beef, he could sometimes be heard in the kitchen singing to the top of his lungs in Chinese as he skilfully swung his huge long-handled cleaver through the bones, dissecting the meat. He told the girls in the café he was singing love songs to his wife. "You expect me to believe that? Don't you be so foolish, Ken, my son. If you were picking flowers, I could see it, but not when you're chopping up meat," Hearsey joked.

He roared at that and said jokingly, "Hearsey, you clazy. Go feed the fish . . . go feed the fish. No, don't go feed the fish . . . fish clazy, too." He would roar once again, impressed with his own jokes. He liked to tease her. His sense of humour did come to the surface from time to time.

However, Ken displayed a level of irritability that drew attention to himself, and for no apparent reason. Some of his behaviour over time was disconcerting and troubling to customers and people in the neighbourhood, leading many to think that he had some mental issues. Edgar Buckley, the café handyman, found Ken unusual. He too had witnessed father and son constantly at one another, not physically, but with raised voices and sometimes shouting in both English and Chinese. One day in October, he was upstairs doing some general repairs and saw a knife under Ken's pillow. Another time he saw a knife under the daybed in the sitting room. They were ugly knives with blades about twenty inches long. These were no ordinary knives but were meant to do serious damage. They were about two inches wide with a square end. The handle had a guard around it that reminded him of a sabre. It was razor sharp and might be used for cutting cane or jungle foliage, or even butchering. Buckley had never seen anything like it in his life, and the sight of it gave him the shivers.

He noticed, too, that sometimes Ken would give bars and candy to the children but, some days, depending on his mood, would not take money or at least appeared to not take money, because it certainly didn't show up in the cash register. This angered Jim, who accused Ken of being lazy and crazy and not doing his part to build the business. He was becoming afraid that the business was failing. Business had dropped off, as some of the regulars were going elsewhere due to their bickering.

Unlike Jim, Ken had no friends apart from Hearsey Canning. Instead of drawing people to him, he frightened people away. Sometimes when young females, including Carol Ann and Juanita Thompson, Malvina and Margaret Elliott, and others came in the store, Ken would place an ice cream bucket full of rocks on the counter, climb up, and then throw them toward the girls one at a time. He used to shout out, "You look like chickens when I cut your head off." This terrified them. This was not good for business in general. Perhaps this was a reference to the constant chatter going on once they came in. The acoustics were poor in the place, and on times it could get very noisy. Many girls felt the psychological scars of his strange behavior for a lifetime. It seemed a bizarre way for Ken to find entertainment.

Meanwhile, Ken couldn't stand the sailors who came to the café, especially the Germans, and the store was known to close when certain ships came into port, to avoid confrontations. This was particularly true of the German boats.

Ken often chased the neighbourhood boys up the tracks and scared the hell out of them, too. The relationship that was once so strong with Jim had been severely sabotaged by Ken's behaviour.

Des Simon, a Burt's Lane boy, was traumatized by Ken and felt that he was a bit crazy and not to be trusted. At best he was unpredictable and definitely not likeable. Being chased with a long-bladed knife was a terrifying experience for anyone, let alone a ten-year-old child. Ken went out more often than Jim to go to the mail or Frank Adams's store. If there was a movie on, he slicked up his hair and dressed up with his long pointed boots, which was a style previously not seen around there. He could look suave at times. Everyone agreed that, without question, Ken was different, to say the least.

Mr. and Mrs. Tom Chow (Tom Yetfoo), and Yvonne (Ah Wan Tse) were owners of the Taiwan Restaurant in Grand Falls, and parents to daughter May Soo. They enjoyed travelling to

Botwood on Sundays. Mrs. Chow had come to Grand Falls, Newfoundland, in 1956. Sunday was the day of the week the Harbourview Cafe was often closed for business, and this gave them time to socialize with Ken and his father, Jim. This visit often included Victor and Boey Chee Wong of the Victory Cafe.

On these occasions, Ken was very kind to them. Ken's specialty was beef jerky, and he always made sure there was extra for his guests to take with them on their return trip home. For some reason Ken was so taken with Tom Chow that on a return visit to Windsor to visit Tom Chow's father, Harry, he gave Tom a gift of a magnificent silk scarf, in those times of very little money. The scarf remains a treasured keepsake of the Chow family to this very day.

May Soo and Don Tom in Grand Falls. Courtesy of May Soo.

During some return visits to the Globe Restaurant in Windsor on Sundays, Jim enjoyed playing a special kind of poker called mah-jong with his friend, the well-known and highly respected Harry Chow, and others. The game required four players, and though Jim enjoyed the game, Ken was not a gambler. However, he enjoyed the fellowship of it all. He would excuse himself and leave the building to return a short while later with a load of treats that could only be described as extremely generous. The game was long, and a special meal would follow at its conclusion, before Jim and his son were heading back to Botwood, refreshed.

Jim's Chinese visitors included Botwood residents and others from out of town. They came to the café and chatted with Jim, and on occasion their spouses came along to these meetings, which were brief but very friendly. These meetings always took place in the dining area, never upstairs. Guests included William Fong, Victor Wong, Mok Yeung, Charlie Chang, Harry Chow, and Tom Chow. In addition, he also had visitors from Buchans, Corner Brook, and Stephenville. Everything was always quite cordial between the Lings and all of his friends.

One of Ken's main shortcomings was his poor command of English. Thankfully, when Hearsey came to work at the café, she approached him all on her own to help him to learn the language. She knew Jim was impatient with Ken because of his poor English, so she thought it would help them both to fix that problem. She looked around home and found some primary school textbooks which she felt would be a great help. Words were often accompanied with pictures to help convey the meaning. It worked like a charm.

Ken was an eager student and a fast learner. Soon he was as fluent as Jim and even surpassed him. Hearsey's graciousness was rewarded with the high regard Ken extended to her at every opportunity, often sitting with her at mealtimes, something he would never do if Jim were around. Father and son sometimes could barely tolerate one another and shunned each other constantly, a torturous way for them to live. But Jim was very pleased at Ken's progress, and Hearsey said to him one day, "Jim, I'd be happy to help you, too, if you would like."

"Yes, Hearsey, I would like that very much. You are good teacher. Soon I speak English as good as Newfoundlander." Then he paused with a twinkle in his eye. She got it. They both roared at his little harmless dig. Soon his language skills were improving as well. Not long afterwards, out of the blue he began referring to her as "Boey," which Hearsey thought meant "boy." This good-looking blonde lady was anything but a boy. She was a looker, all right, and had a steady boyfriend.

"Good enough with me. If that's what he wants to call me, I'm okay with that." She didn't realize that Jim had elevated her status and was regarding her now in the sense that one views a daughter. He watched over her, checking to see that she was okay and no harm was coming her way, even calling to see that she got home okay. While she was not his adopted child, as was

Ken, she brought much to Jim's life and helped fill a void. She had demonstrated "filial respect" without even realizing it. He chose to acknowledge that by ascribing to her a Chinese name. Victor Wong's wife was named Boey, and he liked that name. Mrs. Wong was a very kind and personable individual, and Hearsey had similar characteristics. He would call her Boey. It was perfect. The respect Ken and Jim displayed toward Hearsey was plain for all to see.

12

During lunch one day, right after an English lesson, Jim confided in Hearsey that he did not receive the respect to which he was entitled from his son, as was the custom in China. One day he had mentioned this to Dr. Hugh Twomey as well, and he received a sympathetic ear. It was this treatment that led to conflict between them, he explained. He wanted to ensure that Hearsey understood the reasons behind the tension in the café. Over time she witnessed this conflict in the building, slowly causing it to move from a destination of sanctuary for men and teenagers to a place to be avoided. Disagreements would on times erupt between them, but they were both good to her and to outsiders. In that regard, it was as if they were from different worlds.

Jim's dependence on Hearsey was revealed when one day she told him that she and her fiancé were going to marry in November of 1958, and therefore she would be moving to Norway. Upon hearing this startling news, he said the strangest thing. Jim asked her to postpone it for a year. He even suggested she write and ask her fiancé to sell his home and come to Botwood to live with her. Then he blurted out, "I love you, Hearsey Canning. If you get married and go to Norway and are unhappy and want to return, just let me know. I pay for you to come home. Your job is always waiting."

When she gave it further thought, she realized that his was not a love interest in her at all but rather a reflection of his loneliness and the absence of a female in his life. She was the only woman in his life, and he cared for her as one did for a daughter.

This piece of news rattled him so badly it brought forth these unusual comments. Jim was a delicate man when it came to such matters. Hearsey planned to keep this in mind in the future, as he had much on his mind and she did not want to add to his burdens. She was convinced that he was on the verge of, or in the middle of, a breakdown. There was just so much going on in his life.

Over the months, as Jim pondered his dilemma, he finally resolved to change his position regarding Ken's marital situation. He suggested to Ken that he encourage his wife to reconsider moving to Botwood with her son. He would find a way for renovations to be made to the café, or some other accommodations could be considered. This, Jim believed, would do much to calm their disagreements and, more importantly, would do much to put his long-range family plans back on track. Having a grandchild in his life was a priority.

Ken agreed to discuss this with his wife. She heard him out but was not enthusiastic about such a move. Under current conditions she, being the gentle soul she was, was certainly not ready yet and even went so far as to suggest they move away altogether, preferably to Montreal, where they could start over. She was becoming more and more agitated with their dysfunctional marital arrangement and told him so. But honouring his obligation to Jim meant a great deal to Ken, and so he was further conflicted. This discussion did nothing to relieve his tormented state of mind. In fact, it added fuel to the flames.

Hoping that Ah Yee would join them in Botwood, Jim Ling set his sights on a bride for himself, and in early 1958 he wrote to Hong Kong in search of a mail-order bride to complete the family arrangement. He established a pen pal relationship with a woman, which led to an acceptance on her part to come to Botwood marry him. Her plans were to come a little later, though, around late October or November. She was a gorgeous lady, and Jim proudly displayed her picture and the letter of accepting his proposal to Ken and some of the local young women, who were pleased for Jim's good fortune.

The Confucius belief system to which Jim so adamantly adhered was not a new concept to Ken. He was quite familiar with how things were done. This expectation on Jim's part was an accepted part of Chinese life everywhere. The rage he felt for such betrayal weighed so heavily on Jim that, try as he might, it manifested itself in occasional outbursts of anger directed toward Ken.

This conflict between them gradually began to wear Jim down. Jim's behaviour toward his customers, his friends, and the neighbourhood kids began to change. On occasion he was known to chase some of the young ones away in a moment of frustration, which shocked and frightened them. His sometimes short fuse became even shorter as he continually whined and complained about Ken and openly called him lazy and crazy, right in his presence.

Sometimes after a flare-up between them, Ken would go to bed and stay there, for as long as three days. He just stayed there speaking to no one and making himself absent from all café activities, a behaviour exhibited by Jim himself, oddly enough, on occasion over the years. This annoyed Jim. When Ken withdrew, someone had to take up the slack, and that someone was Jim. Things said in front of customers hurt Ken deeply when it got back to him, and he would lash out in protest about these insults, often resulting in yet another all-out shouting match.

It was odd that Jim could not see himself in Ken. Over the years, he, had himself retreated to his room, sometimes for days, until it passed. His view of himself was not of someone lazy or crazy but rather of a person overwhelmed. How was Ken so different? Was he not yearning for a warm bed to share with Ah Yee, his beautiful wife, and to enjoy life with Don Tom? The parallels between the two were many. Perhaps Jim would eventually see the light and take a softer position regarding Ken and be more compassionate toward him. The disappointment and disrespect Ken brought weighed heavy on Jim, and he struggled to accept it and forgive.

One day, Jim was having a bad day, annoyed with Ken, when in came Ray Lidstone, a regular who considered himself a friend. Ray sometimes used to carry on with him, and Jim would tolerate it and actually enjoy the banter. It was two years after Ken's arrival, and they'd had a wicked argument earlier that morning. But on this particular visit, as Ray was carrying on as per normal with Jim, he unexpectedly launched into a rage. In a flash, Jim grabbed a full unopened bottle of Coke and slung it with all his might toward Ray from twenty feet away. It narrowly missed his head and bounced off a booth. Jim shouted, "No respect. Ray Lidstone. You get out my store! Go feed the fish." Ray left, startled and shivering with fear.

Had the bottle connected, severe damage could have been done, even death. Ray really considered Jim his friend and was both frightened and hurt inside at the outburst. He came back the next day and sincerely apologized, but from this time going forward he had an amended attitude. He would never tease Jim again. Damage done. Lesson learned. Times were changing, and so was Jim.

Sometimes Ken and Jim's arguing and cursing each other up in both English and Chinese happened right in the café, right in front of customers. Hearsey had witnessed Ken doing some strange things. It was enough to convince her that they actually hated one another.

On a couple of occasions when she and Ken happened to be in the kitchen at the same time, she saw Ken point a knife at his father's back. One of those times happened the first week in October 1958, and the other around October 24. On those occasions Ken would be cutting vegetables in the kitchen and his father would come in for a drink of water. When his back would turn, Ken would point the knife in the direction of Jim's back and bring the point to within a foot of his father. When these episodes took place, Hearsey would leave the kitchen immediately.

Ken would take pokers and place them in the stove and brandish them about to threaten misbehaving juveniles, who were driving him mad on occasion. While he never used them, he told Hearsey straight out that if they came in the kitchen he would not hesitate to do so.

On Sunday, October 12, Hearsey witnessed a strange thing

that really frightened her. Jim asked a bunch of boys to leave, as they had been tormenting him by running around the café. Once they were out the door, they turned and began to throw stones through the open door. Jim reacted and threw bottles at them in a savage manner, intent on injuring them. He really meant business. It was the first time she had seen him behave this crazily. As Jim was closing the café door, Ken quietly walked up behind him. Behind Ken's back she clearly saw an axe in his hand. He just crept over and stood very close to his father, whereupon he raised the axe above his head. She could not be certain if he intended to bring it down on Jim or not, but when he did swing it downward, it caught on the door as it was closing. It was a very close call. Ken had come close to the edge. She couldn't help but notice that tension between the two had been steadily escalating.

Later that week, something else quite weird took place in the evening. Sometimes Jim did things spontaneously, which left many, including his friends, confused or even shocked. He often used to have some friends over from time to time, especially his extremely good friend and next-door neighbour, Frank Adams.

One evening while regulars were gathered around the table playing cards, somehow a tomcat got in the café. Like lightning, and in anger at the interruption, Jim grabbed it, lifted the lid of the red-hot stove, threw the animal in and banged the lid shut. Goodbye cat.

Everything stopped as Frank and others looked on in shock. Upset, they spoke up about it. Jim was confused at the reaction. As if nothing had happened, he said, "Whose deal?" It would be the last time Frank Adams would play cards at the café, although they would remain friends. Things were really getting crazy at the café, and it was the talk of the town.

By now Jim had been looking forward longingly to the arrival of his future wife, which would be happening any time soon. Their letters had become more frequent, and at Jim's request, Hearsey had read letters he had exchanged with her through the Immigration office. He was ecstatic at the prospects.

Such was his joy that he had shown her picture to other young female customers, who were struck by her beauty. "I never saw anyone in my life as beautiful as that young woman," said Marie Wells. Jim placed every confidence in Hearsey in regard to these exchanges, and she was very excited for her employer. *Soon his loneliness will vanish once and for all*, she thought.

Hearsey couldn't wait to get home to tell the wonderful news. Linda, her niece, was there at the time. Although six years younger than she, Linda was mature for her age and became her companion and source of support on many occasions. Often she would visit her aunt at the café and go with her to the Dew Drop Inn, a teenage hangout on Circular Road, after work.

There she spoke her mind to everyone there. "You know, I certainly hope this woman who's coming is gentle. Jim is so soft and tender and kind to everyone. He needs someone just like that to bring him happiness. He's got enough rowdiness in his life right now with Ken. He certainly doesn't need any more." They all agreed and anxiously waited for her arrival in November. They were filled with compassion for Jim the Chinaman.

Meanwhile, Jim had become more and more accepting of the fact that Ken was married and discussed the situation on numerous occasions with Ken. Jim again suggested that it could be a happy place to raise their child if they worked on it together. Jim knew what loneliness was and felt his son shouldn't have to live like that. No one should. Ken was surprised at Jim's reaction and commenced corresponding with his wife regarding this new development. There was much to consider, not the least of which was the accommodations in the café. They were not ideal for a husband and wife. It would require further modifications, or the couple would have to live in a separate dwelling. Nonetheless, there were possibilities. This helped dissipate some tension between the two, and Jim was liking the idea. Perhaps this might work out after all.

In light of this, Hearsey would say to Jim, "You're in denial about Ken."

"What you mean, Hearsey?" he said in reply.

"Well, you sometimes say that you hate him and wish he would go away, and here you are encouraging him to bring his wife over. Maybe you've had a change of heart. If you have, then great. All four of you can have a wonderful life in Botwood, especially when your own bride arrives in November."

Jim grinned and went back to reading his paper. "Perhaps you are right," he said, and began to envision a happy family life together right there in Botwood.

March 31, 1949, was a historic day for Canada. Its provinces numbered ten on that date when Newfoundland, England's oldest colony, by virtue of the results of a referendum, and by the narrowest of margins, saw its population vote for union with Canada. It was a virtual tie, and many felt that somehow it was rigged and still think so today. It had been intended to make April 1 the date of signing, but Premier Smallwood would never have it said that we joined Canada on April Fool's Day.

Regardless, Canadians we became, albeit with a unique history and needing policing tied to the federal system. The Newfoundland Constabulary would be policing St. John's while the RCMP would handle the rest of the province. The Rangers would be assimilated into the federal force, along with some of the Newfoundland Constabulary, and posted to the outports. Certain responsibilities of the Rangers were removed to enable justice matters to be more efficiently applied. While St. John's was the main division, Corner Brook in 1954 would become a subdivision answerable to St. John's, and Botwood was one of the towns that fell under the responsibility of Corner Brook.

Terry Hoey was blessed to grow up in a happy family in Peterborough, Ontario. His mom, Jean, was a devout Roman Catholic. She made sure that all of her nine children attended St. Peter's regularly and participated in all other church activities, including raising funds for the construction of a new church. The existing facility was old and beyond repair. The Hoey children were or would become engaged in a wide range of trades, including drafting, electrical, accounting, bricklaying, and sales. Terry loved Canadian football, about which most Newfoundlanders knew little or nothing. Newfoundlanders preferred soccer, broomball, softball, and hockey. But hockey was the big attraction in Terry's hometown, and the Montreal Canadiens farm team, the Peterborough Petes, coached by Scotty Bowman, was his favourite team. Peterborough, like Botwood, was a very safe and secure place in which to grow up, and Terry considered settling down there. His outgoing personality attracted many friends to his world, including the girls, who were smitten by his good looks and charm. Upon completion of high school at St. Peter's, he tried a number of jobs. He secured a job as city assessor for a brief period. However, his strong faith led him to seriously consider becoming a priest. It was not unusual to come home to find him with a number of priests engaged in theological discussions of religion.

Left: RCMP Officer J. Terrance Hoey.
Right: Terry Hoey at Regina.
Photos courtesy of Patricia Fryer.

Terry stood over six feet tall, and some would say he was Hollywood handsome. He just enjoyed the attention his looks brought and joked about it good-naturedly, as any young man would. But he was just not happy with his work as an assessor. In particular, the wages were not great, and he wanted to help his mom with the upkeep of her home. It was one huge family for a single parent to raise. Try as he might, Terry just couldn't decide what he wanted to do, and then one day it happened. A friend dropped by, a recent graduate from Regina's RCMP Depot, and he was hooked. In short order he was heading across Canada for mandatory training.

It was into Newfoundland's remarkable history this young Mountie from M Troop rode in October of 1958. This Peterborough native saw the posting dated October 7, showing he was being sent to "B" Division in St. John's, Newfoundland, along with some of his friends. John Terrance Hoey was filled with ex-

Terry Hoey (left) and fellow officers. Courtesy of Patricia Fryer.

cited expectation as he said his farewells to his mother and sister Barbara at the graduation. Jean Hoey's final words of advice to her young son were, "Careful, Terry, you're in a dangerous job." With that, he and several other graduates, including Artie Daye, Royce Getson, John Brayley, and others, eagerly boarded the

FRED HUMBER

Terry Hoey, Jean Hoey (mother), and sister Barbara at RCMP graduation. Photos courtesy of Patricia Fryer.

The original Spot Cash in Botwood. Courtesy of Nancy Fong.

train headed east. Following a terrifying ferry ride on the *William Carson* and an incredible train ride on the "Newfie Bullet," they were introduced to their commanding officer, Inspector Arthur Argent. A few hours later, they were at Windsor Station, and from there on to Botwood. Plans to station him at St. John's had changed. He was informed on the train that he would instead be posted to Botwood.

Hoey was fortunate in finding accommodations at Rita Langdon's boarding house, immediately across from Charlie Chang's Spot Cash. He had arrived at last, exhausted and ready to go to work.

13

The next morning at 9:00 a.m., just as stores were being opened, Terry Hoey stopped into Charlie's Spot Cash. A young and beautiful Dot Lidstone was on duty.

"You're new around here, aren't you, my son? Don't remember seeing you before," she greeted him.

"Yes," said Terry. "I just moved in next door at the boarding house. I'm Terry Hoey, from Peterborough, Ontario. As you can see, I'm a Mountie and am starting work here today."

"Oh, you mean Reets. You'll get along with her just fine. Everyone does. She's a great cook. And never mind that you're a mainlander. Sure, everyone's welcome around here. Now, my son, what can I do for you?"

He's just such a charming young fellow, she thought, *and almost as handsome as Bill.*

"I'd like a pack of Players Light, please," he said, and then off he went out the door, on his way to his first day of work.

Bill Butler was Dorothy's fiancé and would have a major part to play in events awaiting the young fellow from Peterborough.

A similar scene would play itself out every day at the same time, like clockwork, including that fateful morning of November 6. Dot remembered it clearly. Always the Players Light, every single morning.

Soon Terry would be introduced to a young woman who happened to be a sister to James Gill, Meriam's husband. She was a knockout, like something that just stepped off the silver screen. They both thought they would make a splendid couple. The two would become friends but were not ready for a serious relationship. After all, they were both so young and there was so much life to be lived.

DEATH AT THE HARBOURVIEW CAFE

Constable Terry Hoey regularly wrote home to bring his siblings up-to-date and encourage them to work hard in school. It didn't take him long to notice that many young people in Botwood had left school without completing grade eleven to take menial jobs or just hang out around town. To him, the future of the dropouts didn't appear too bright. *Why sell yourself short like that?* he wondered.

On Wednesday, October 15, 1958, which coincidentally was Terry Hoey's first day on the job, the SS *Alstertal* arrived at 11:00 a.m. with a cargo of sulphur. She tied up to the ore wharf and started to off-load the product to be sent by rail to the mill at Grand Falls.

Ore wharf. Courtesy of Alan Thomas.

During her stay, some of the crew members, like crews of other vessels of various nationalities, just hung out around town, going to movies and restaurants, and drinking beer at the Legion or the Argyle tavern. Among them were several large, boisterous sailors who soon developed reputations as agitators, just spilling for a racket, while some younger members of the crew who tagged along were simply innocent kids, some on their very first trip away from home and just enjoying life.

At the time the ship came around, Killick Island, preparing to dock, an RCMP cruiser was crossing the tarmac on what remained of the military base. Inside were Constable Hannon, commanding officer of the Botwood detachment, and Constable Terry Hoey, the rookie. Hannon smiled and thought of his training days there and looked forward to be heading back soon to Regina to do another course. He was giving young Hoey a brief tour of the town when he caught sight of a black vessel flying a German flag, steaming past Killick Island, headed for the ore wharf. Hannon told Hoey, "The ships usually have Norwegian, British, or Greek crews, and there is seldom any trouble with them, except for a few rackets with the locals over girls." But the Germans could generally be counted on to stir things up, as on occasion they could be quite aggressive.

Over the next few days, Hoey would be accompanied by either Constable Bowen, known as "Red," for obvious reasons, who had been posted to Botwood for two years, or by Constable Robert Healey from Grand Falls, commanding officer temporarily assigned as Hannon's replacement. Red was well liked by the locals, especially the family of Art Thompson, and by Jim Ling in particular, who had developed an excellent rapport with the Mountie. One or the other would show Hoey the shoreline leading to Fortune Harbour, the branch road going to Leading Tickles.

Terry Hoey's second day on the job, October 16, was routine. The morning brought a meeting at the station, which included First Constable Hannon, Second Constable Bowen, and Third Constable Hoey, to ensure that everyone was up-to-date regarding various complaints that had been made to the detachment, for possible investigation and follow-up. These included some fishing violations and thefts in Fortune Harbour, and an assault in Cottrell's Cove. Further, a suspected case of arson and the illegal sale of liquor was reported in Leading

Tickles and Glover's Harbour. Things were pretty quiet out around the bay.

On Saturday night, October 18, there was a hockey game in Grand Falls. It was sure to be exciting, since the Corner Brook Royals were in town to play the ANDCOs. The place was buzzing with excitement as fans streamed out from Botwood on the company caboose, the Nickle Train, the Red Wing Bus, or by carpooling or hitchhiking.

Art Thompson invited Terry Hoey to accompany his family to the game. Art assured him it would be worth the trip. "That bunch from Corner Brook with what's-their-names—Danky Dorrington, Cloby Collins, Orin Carver, Jim Grant, and Frank Walsh—my son, they're going to get it tonight."

Art railed on, "That crowd is no match for our team. Wes Trainor, Ollie Tulk, Jim Barker, Jim Kennedy, Ralph Cook, the very cagey and temperamental Roger Dean from Botwood, and that Vic Grignon, the man who could break off boards with his slapshot. By the way, Terry, bring along a tie. We are going to the Oasis after the game for a scuff."

Terry enjoyed the game as much as he enjoyed the crazy fans hanging from the steel rafters directly over the players' benches. The hockey game put his mind right back home in Peterborough and their coach, Scotty Bowman, who would in time go down in history as one of the most successful coaches in the NHL. Right now, he was watching this young black Collins fellow from Nova Scotia strut his stuff. Terry was impressed with the fact that fans on both sides cheered his moves.

In the early evening of Tuesday, October 21, some of the crew from the SS *Alstertal* came into the Harbourview Cafe, as they often did to order food and just hang out. Some of them had been drinking earlier down on their ship, just across the road, and were half cut. One was particularly intoxicated. As the evening progressed, he became loud and obnoxious in an otherwise pleasant atmosphere. Local teenagers were also present, ordering up their Cokes and chips, and listening to their favourite tunes on the jukebox.

Buddy Holly was coming on the scene, and everyone liked to go to Jim's for a dance and a chat. Jim permitted that just as long as it didn't interfere with business. The crowd often included Eleanor Horwood, Marie Wells, Jeannette Boone, Maxine Stuckless, Sandra Pelley, and several of the Waterman girls: Deanna, Jean, and Marion. Everything was going great, with nearly all of the thirteen booths occupied, with teenagers chatting about things like King Creole, the latest Elvis movie, or where they were going for Bonfire Night. Otherwise they were putting an occasional coin in the jukebox and having a dance to "Splish Splash," "Peggy Sue," or "Great Balls of Fire."

"The Punt." Old punts would often be burned on Bonfire Night.
Courtesy of artist Clifford George.

The mood began to change, ever so slowly at first. It began when this very young drunk German fellow, who for the purposes of this narrative the author will call Gunther. He was one of the crowd that had come in from the ship, and he decided to make his way over to the jukebox and load it with coins. He then selected this new song that Gordon Locke had just put in a week ago. It was brand new, a release called "Western Movies." He liked the song so much he punched in the number twenty times or so.

The song began to play over and over, causing a murmur of disapproval from the teenagers. "What in the hell is buddy doing? Sure, you can't dance to that."

"Not only that, I don't like that song. We've heard it five times already, and it's driving me nuts. If he don't knock that off, I'm going over there and yank out the plug."

"Don't do that, b'y. That might cause a racket, and he'll put the place up. You can see he's loaded."

The song started again, and Ken came dashing from the kitchen. "You clazy in the head? Play too much same song, people not like. Play another song, please." Satisfied that he had made his point, Ken returned to the kitchen to fill the orders.

Gunther was having a good time and was not the least concerned about Ken. He kept leaning over the jukebox, looking in at the record spinning. There was one place in the song which had sound effects of gunshots, where the singer sang, "Shoot 'em up, my baby loves Western movies," to the sound of bullets going off rapid-fire. Gunther would spin to his right and madly flail his arms around, screaming at the top of his lungs, pretending to be shooting off imaginary pistols.

After a brief reprieve, the song would restart and provide Gunther an opportunity for a repeat performance. He was becoming more exaggerated each time. He knew Ken had very little patience, having been in the café nearly every day since he came into port. After three more performances, tempers began to flare. Everyone's nerves were rubbed raw, worst of all Ken's. It seemed obvious to all that Gunther was doing this just to aggravate him. To no one's surprise, Ken came out once more, and this time he told Gunther to select another song or he would have to leave, and with that he returned to the kitchen.

The song spun twice more, and in the middle of the third spin, Ken stormed out, by now a wild man.

In a shrill voice, and pointing his finger and tapping at his own head, Ken screamed, "You clazy in the head? You get out now. Go feed the fish! Go feed the fish!" Ken reached for the wall socket and angrily snatched the plug from the wall. What a relief that was for everyone when silence prevailed. It was a rare moment when everyone felt like shaking Ken's hand.

Everyone except Gunther.

The silence seemed to last forever. Ken was erratic enough most of the time without someone egging him on. This time there was no doubt in anyone's mind. He had been pushed to the limit.

Gunther and his crewmates went berserk. They grabbed wooden cases of Coca-Cola empties and began to throw them around. Broken glass flew everywhere, and the wooden cases damaged the building. The police were called, but not before there was considerably more damage. It spoiled the night for everyone.

Jim and Ken, left with the mess to clean up, were understandably upset.

Constables Bowen and Hoey arrived on the scene in about a half-hour to take statements, but not before the German crew members had retreated to the safety of the *Alstertal*. Jim already had enough problems and didn't need this issue to deal with, especially when the health department was due to make an inspection in a couple of days. Warrick Swyers usually had compliance matters pertaining to the café he wanted dealt with, making his visits something to be dreaded. When asked if he wished to press charges for the damages, Jim replied, "No, but thanks, Red, for showing up so quickly. No one was hurt."

Early the next evening, October 22, the young German crew came back to the café to apologize for what had happened the previous evening. This included Gunther, who had been the cause of the fuss. On the captain's instructions, they were to smooth out the situation before the ship sailed in a few days. After all, if this was going to be a regular port of call for the *Alstertal*, then hostility was the last thing he wanted to have to deal with each time they returned. Having recently been appointed as captain, pressure from the owners regarding incidents dealing with immigration and the law would put his job in jeopardy. He was quite prepared to fire the goddamn works of those who had been involved.

Most of the local regulars were there again the night the crew turned up to apologize. Jim was over on the eastern side of the café working on some tax papers.

As they walked up by the kitchen, Ken, who was inside preparing a meal, spotted them. He and Jim had spent a lot of the day straightening up the mess from the previous night and giving statements to the police. And here these bastard Germans were, back again. Goddamn. He was in a blood-red rage. In his hatred of these sailors, he had the belief there was going to be more violence. He reacted instantly. Like lightning, saying nothing, he turned and ran back into the kitchen. Ken was taking no more bullshit from them. He'd had more than enough. He had more important issues on his mind than them.

In the kitchen, he had been making french fries in preparation for the usual evening orders. He grabbed the pan of hot fat from the stove and ran back out. He lunged toward them, screaming wildly, and slung the pan in their direction.

The fat landed directly in Gunther's face. He was just a young kid, perhaps eighteen or nineteen. His face melted on the spot. He became unrecognizable. It only took a second or two. It was a moment in time, really, still talked about to this day with disbelief, sadness, and overriding compassion.

Sadly, the flying superheated fat struck him point-blank in the face and eyes, causing severe burns. He shrieked again and again, in agony and fright, and started racing around the café blindly. A tall, heavy-set crew member reached out and grabbed the boy.

He shouted, "I've got you, Gunther. I've got you. It's okay! We are taking you to the hospital. Hang on, Gunther, hang on."

The café fell silent. Not a whisper from the local teenagers. They listened as Jim frantically called the hospital, whereupon Ken Dean and his stake-body truck were on the scene in minutes, along with a doctor. From there Gunther and two crew members were transported to the local hospital, where staff scrambled to provide emergency care.

Jim stood there, shaken to the core, at a loss for words. Regaining some composure, he screamed out at Ken, "Get the hell upstairs! Son of a bitch, son of a bitch!" Ken raced upstairs, taking three steps at a time. Jim's mind was racing. What had Ken just done? Last night's fight was bad enough, but now the damage to this young sailor would surely bring the full weight of the law and the Department of Immigration officials down on him as well. There was no way he or Ken could dodge this bullet. Would Ken be sent to jail? Would he be deported? Would the financial costs of damages to this poor young sailor be the end of the Harbourview Cafe? Ken was surely a crazy man, crazy in the head. His son was crazy, no doubt about it.

Jim spoke to the patrons in a rambling fashion, still trembling, "I am sorry, but must close the café now. Police soon be here. Thank you for coming." The patrons filed out, everyone shocked at the sudden explosion of violence and horror they had just witnessed. The news spread like wildfire throughout the Caucasian and Chinese community, to the dismay of all concerned. No one had seen this coming.

Hearsey had not realized how the behaviour of the Lings affected the Chinese community as a whole. The Chinese had invested a tremendous amount of effort to blend into the general population, with great success. The ancients stressed the smooth functioning of society as opposed to individualism. Peace and contentment were highly valued. Drawing negative attention to themselves was something they did not need, and with all the goings-on at the café since Ken's arrival, there was an abundance of that. But prior episodes at the café had found a way to peaceful resolution with calm intervention from the renowned Harry Chow, among others. It was only a matter of time and this, too, would go away.

Gunther remained in hospital for several days, until arrangements could be made for him to go to St. John's, where specialists in plastic surgery would attend him. He had undergone a frightening transformation, and the community was quite shaken up, as it was rumoured that he may have lost his sight. Understandably, the situation was such that charges were to be laid and compensation sought. In St. John's, immigration officials and lawyers were mobilized to deal with the legalities from the perspective of the ship's owners, the company, the captain, and the victim, all of which would filter down to Jim. Yet more problems to add to the pressure cooker.

Dorm Parsons explained, "You know it was too bad all 'round. The Germans were good to us young people, you know. When they came to port, they used to buy us Cokes and spent money on us without us asking. They seemed to have lots of money and knew we did not and were kind to us. What more can I say? That incident with Ken ruined everything, and that poor German kid. . . . What happened to him in the end, I wonder?"

And Jim's troubles continued to mount. At 2:00 p.m. on Thursday, October 23, the local health inspector, Warrick Swyers, went to the Harbourview Cafe to deliver a long list of complaints and health violations. These had evolved over a long period of time, with failures to comply, including messy floors, dirty bathrooms, the occasional roaming cat wandering in from the street, and the unfinished bathroom upstairs. Swyers's visit was totally unrelated to the fight and the fat-throwing incident, which had occurred the previous two nights. What an unfortunate coincidence for Jim, who was still staggering under the pressure of recent events and his own ongoing personal challenges with Ken. The two were still engrossed in their long-standing conflict, with Jim now trying to reach a compromise with him. Ken's attempts to persuade Ah Yee to come to Botwood, rather than calm the waters, seemed to make Ken more agitated, but Jim lived in hope. And Jim's bride-to-be hadn't written to him now for several weeks. This made him anxious.

What is it with Jim? Swyers wondered. *If he would just clean the place up and repair the washrooms like I have instructed him to do, then things would be just fine and the drastic news I have today would be unnecessary.*

Swyers was married to Ruth Jewer, who grew up in Botwood on Coronation Street, just one street over from their current home. She was a sister to Nelson Jewer, Jim's good friend, who worked at Montreal Shipping. The Swyers family liked the town so much that they chose to reside there, in spite of the fact that his office was located twenty miles away in Grand Falls.

Warrick's face was a familiar one to Jim. He recalled his first visit there. At that time there had been some minor infractions requiring attention, but not enough to shut the business down. Giving him deadlines was like pouring water on a duck's back. It would get worse. In May and June of 1958, there were follow-up visits and notes made of further infractions of the health code regulations, and instructions given along with completion dates, so much so that back in August he felt there was no alternative, but to close the food-preparation component of the café. Due to work pressures, Warrick was unable to go to see Jim to tell him the bad news. Until today, this day of all days, the day following the issues with the German sailors. It was a visit Jim could have done without. Taking no chances, Swyers had requested a police officer make the call with him. This fell to Constable Terry Hoey. This was the rookie's third response to the business in three days, having been called there the night the *Alstertal*'s crew trashed the place and after the following night's horrific incident with Gunther.

A still shaken Jim did not take the inspector's news well. It was a terrible blow for the business, as it was the most important income source of the café. Now all he could sell were soft drinks and confectionery and smokes. Jim's eyes began to water with the news. "No, no, no! This is no good, Swyers. Business depend on kitchen."

He pleaded to Swyers, but to no avail. He had abused the man's good nature and disregarded the law. Jim called his lawyer, Mr. J. C. Higgins, and also Magistrate Cramm, both of whom he knew well, and explained the situation, with promises to comply as soon as possible. While these men were sympathetic, there was a process to follow and consequences if you did not heed it. The health of the public trumped everything else. Jim needed an immediate reprieve, and it was not forthcoming.

Suddenly, without any warning, he was having trouble

breathing and his mind began to spin. For a moment the pressure sent his thoughts back in time to when he attempted suicide at the Immigration office. Could he hold out and not go bankrupt? Was this the end of his dream? He knew there was very little cash in the safe and even less in the bank. If only Ken would stop giving away confectionary to the children and get them to pay, as he should, but no, Ken just ignored him. Why did he hide away in his room for days sometimes and not help with the work? How come people who were once regular customers were no longer coming? Perhaps he should cut back on his gambling. Even though he was desperate for answers, Jim regained control and was able to calm himself down.

He decided, as a partial and immediate cash-flow solution, that he would do two things. First, he would withhold Hearsey's wages for a couple of weeks, but he would make it up to her. He loved that young woman for what she brought to the business: her smile, her kindness, and genuine interest in both him and that miserable Ken, who was single-handedly ruining his life. She was one of a kind, and he blushed with embarrassment for what he was now about to do to someone who had shown him only loyalty and compassion. Their relationship was founded upon mutual respect, and he watched over her as one watches over a daughter. He realized that he only paid her wages partially and not the full amount owed, but starting on Saturday he would start withholding her entire pay. He felt he had no choice. Moreover, he would immediately apply the promise he gave Hearsey, to stop gambling altogether, until his finances were once more under control.

Jim spent hours on the phone on the day of October 28, with officials from Immigration and the Justice Department, pertaining to legalities involving Gunther. These would be addressed on the next trip to port of the *Alstertal*, as she was about to depart for the eastern seaboard. That very evening the burly crew members of the *Alstertal*, their ship finally loaded after the long delay, stopped by the café once again with steely eyes glaring and voices raised. Fifteen teenagers looked on as they confronted Jim and Ken in a very matter-of-fact way, face to face.

"Our ship is sailing tomorrow, but we will be back. When we do, we will settle this once and for all. You will die for what you did to Gunther. You have ruined his life. He was just a boy, that's all, just a boy. You will pay." With that they turned, slammed the door behind them, and stomped off into the rainy night, down over the bank and on to their ship.

Jim and Ken were left trembling in fear. So were the young customers. They had heard it all. The sailors meant every word. The ship couldn't leave soon enough.

The *Alstertal* departed Botwood at 3:00 p.m. the next day, Wednesday. The question on everyone's mind was, "When is the *Alstertal* returning?" No one wanted to be in either Ken or Jim's shoes on that day.

Hearsey was aware that Ken had written several times to Ah Yee about the options they had pertaining to she and Don Tom moving to Botwood and thought that perhaps they had made a decision. Unknown to Hearsey, their exchanges over time had gotten heated between the two, as it was obvious this was not a happy or healthy place to raise a child. These letters often led to Ken becoming depressed and desperate and angry at the situation in which he found himself. This most recent example of his rage, having burned a young sailor, was the last straw. The fallout from that incident loomed large. In a messed-up state of mind, he wrote to Ah Yee the day following the incident, holding nothing back. He had had enough. She was to make immediate arrangements to meet him in Montreal with their baby boy. He was leaving. To hell with honour. To hell with it all!

Ah Yee wanted a life with Ken, but the catastrophe he had described at the Harbourview was more than she was prepared to endure. This was a pivotal moment in their lives. His choice was made. There would be no compromise. What a relief! She prepared to depart for Montreal as soon as she could, and her heart was filled with joy.

Things were suddenly crystal clear to Ken. He had one more letter to write that night, to another party. He set to work immediately and left early the next morning for the post office to ensure it reached its destination as quickly as possible.

Around 11 a.m. the next day, Thursday, October 30, Ambrose Ball, one of the inner circle and next-door neighbour of Jim's, stopped by the café for a chat, as he often did. Jim asked, "Is it okay to borrow your .303 Enfield rifle? I am thinking about buying one."

"Sure enough, Jim. I'll drop it off this afternoon on my way to work. Before I take off, can I have a slice of your coconut cream pie?"

"I just baked some a few hours ago. I'll get you a piece. Thank you, Am."

Ambrose left the café shortly after, thinking that he had never known Jim to go hunting. Yes, on occasion he knew Jim shot a few gulls from an upstairs window. But hunting? He dismissed the thought and casually strolled up the lane to his home. He returned around 3:45 p.m. with the gun, passed it directly to Jim, and went down the embankment to the company wharf to start his shift, not giving it another thought.

14

Upon arrival at work one morning, Hearsey spotted the sad face of Jim Ling as he slowly descended the stairway into the empty café.

"Ken has done it this time, Hearsey," said a very unhappy Jim.

"What is it, Jim? What's going on?" Hearsey asked innocently.

"Ken is crazy, crazy in the head. He need to be locked up in hospital. I get Dr. Twomey to certify him insane. No one would blame me. It is all his fault. I not take it anymore," he ranted.

Hearsey went right over to him, looked him straight in the eyes, and asked, "What in God's name are you going on about, Jim? What has Ken done to you?"

"He write letter to my bride. He say I treat him bad and that I am very bad person. She send me letter to say she has changed mind. Not coming now. Not going to marry me. Is very bad, Hearsey. Ken has done very bad thing."

Hearsey was shocked by the news. She knew what it meant to have a woman come into his life and how happy he was—ecstatic, really, that he would have a companion at last. She walked over to him, tenderly touched his arm, and said, "I am so sorry that you have been hurt, Jim. I don't know what to say."

Hearsey Canning.
Courtesy of Hugo Thulgreen.

Jim acknowledged her concern, grabbed the coal shovel, lifted the lid on the stove, and threw some coal in. Tears streaming down his face, he turned and walked away from her and up the stairs to the living quarters, openly weeping by now and muttering, "Why he disrespect me? Why he break my heart?"

He slipped inside the living quarters and quietly shut the door. He needed some time alone to compose himself.

Hearsey stood there, unable to move. Her heart was aching because of what she had just witnessed. "This is not over yet," she said to herself. This is going to get worse before it gets better . . . if it's going to get better."

That part of Jim's dream was gone. The bride would never arrive. But was there anything left to cling to? Yes, there was. At least Ken's wife was going to come over, and soon there would be little ones. Strangely, as days passed, Jim gradually regained his composure.

15

It wasn't until Monday, November 3, that Hearsey Canning realized something very unusual. A whole week had passed since the kitchen had been shut down. At lunchtime she sat at a booth expecting Jim to join her. However, he said, "Me not have lunch today. Me feel sick, perhaps lie down soon." She had come in as usual at 9:00 a.m., and at 3:00 p.m. she asked Jim to allow her to leave early, to get her hair done. Instead of turning his back on her and muttering and stammering, as he often did, he seemed to be very strangely upbeat and actually anxious for her to go.

He said, "Okay with me, Hearsey. Here is three dollars for a hairdo. You have good time tonight, okay Hearsey?"

She couldn't believe her ears. She had never seen this type of behaviour all the while she had worked there. Still, in the back of her mind she wondered why she had not been paid any wages recently. Edgar Buckley, the handyman, was in agreement that both father and son never looked so happy in each other's company since Ken had arrived. What was going on?

This release from despair was what was now being reflected in Ken's demeanour, clearly obvious to everyone. It was true, Hearsey and Buckley had never seen Ken happier. He seemed almost euphoric. Jim's face, too, was considerably relaxed. The scowl so often prevalent when he and Ken were together was noticeably absent. Had Jim forgiven Ken for that brutal, soul-crushing letter he had received from his intended bride, totally attributable to Ken's terrible intrusion in his love life? If so, that was remarkable. Or had Jim, the poor man so laden down with worries, lost his mind completely? In any event, these were blissful moments between the two the likes of which she had never before witnessed.

When she had asked Jim about her outstanding wages, he had gently scolded her, saying, "You spend too much money. You should save more for future." That was the extent of his explanation. She simply accepted that she would be paid soon, whatever was holding things up. She trusted and respected Jim implicitly and knew there must be a good reason. She could wait to get paid.

A little later in the afternoon, Hearsey noticed that Ken was outside, up on the roof at the back, installing barbed wire over the sitting-room window on the top level. Buckley had only finished laying the shingles there a few hours before. This, too, was quite odd, and Mr. Buckley commented that Ken should not be doing it. Ken had put some barbed wire to his own bedroom window a couple of days after the *Alstertal* sailed, and he was now finishing the job. Buckley had never seen anything so weird. After all, barbed wire was usually put up for controlling animals. How weird was that?

Earlier that morning, when Edgar Buckley was in the living quarters adjusting some window framing, Ken came in.

"I'm going to the early movie in Grand Falls tonight. Are you going in?" he asked Ken.

Ken replied, "I'm going to the midnight show, but I'll probably go in early, on the 6:30 bus with you." With that, Ken lifted his suitcase up on his bed and flipped it open.

Seeing that is was filled with neatly pressed clothes, Buckley asked, "Going somewhere?"

"To Montreal," said Ken. "I've got my clothes ironed and packed and will be heading out on Tuesday. I've got to get out of this place. My mind is made up."

Buckley said nothing and went back to his work.

About to leave, Hearsey shrugged and dismissed this unusual behaviour from her mind and finished her chores before heading out to keep her hair appointment with Ches Thornhill. His shop was just two doors away from Frank Adams's store. As she was about to leave, Linda, her niece, came in.

"I thought I'd walk down with you and wait while you get your hair done," said Linda.

"Thanks for being so thoughtful."

Hearsey and Linda left to walk downtown. It was then they overheard Jim and Ken in conversation in the kitchen.

"She not coming!" said Ken. "She not coming!" Very matter-of-fact and intense.

Jim then muttered, "You crazy? She crazy, too?" Hearsey was not sure, but it seemed to be in reference to Ken's wife. Already their voices were taking on a familiar agitated, grating, upward-spiralling tone.

"That spurt of happiness didn't last long," said Hearsey as they continued to walk away, not knowing it would be the last time they would see father and son together. They had heard them argue before. It was just another argument.

A few hours later, around 6:10 p.m., Frank Adams stopped into Jim's on the way home. He had forgotten to take a can of milk with him from his shop and decided to pick one up from Jim.

"Closing early today, Jim?" he asked, having spotted that the two front windows now had their shutters pulled together.

"Yes, Frank. Me feeling sick and need to lie down," Jim replied.

Frank noticed that Ken was inside the kitchen washing dishes and Buckley was preparing to leave.

"If you're going to Grand Falls on the bus, Ken, I'll wait for you," Buckley called out.

Jim answered for him. "Go on by yourself, Edgar. Ken will leave when he's ready."

Noticing a growing impatience on Jim's part to go lie down, Frank and Edgar departed, leaving the two by themselves.

While rarely spoken about openly in the café, the *Alstertal* was due back in port in a few weeks. Around town, talk of the threats made were already circulating. Trouble was coming.

A little later that evening, around 7:00 p.m., some passersby noticed Jim looking drawn and unsmiling as he closed the doors and prepared to shut the café. He was far from happy.

At home, Hearsey, with so much going on, reminisced about the café and her first day on the job. She was only twenty-one, and in no time at all she had come to truly enjoy working there. Among her duties, she was often required to clean the upstairs living quarters, so she knew that part of the building as well as she did the lower café level. Few people were welcome there apart from Frank Adams, Buckley, and herself, so she thought herself privileged.

A stairway led from the western side of the café up to a five-foot-square landing. From the landing it was necessary to turn left and take one step to a new level. Immediately in front was a doorway leading into the living quarters. If instead of entering the living area one turned right, there was a small unfinished bathroom on the immediate right, one of numerous unmet requirements of the health department, past which was a huge display room where Jim kept cases of Haig Ale, empty bottles, and odds and ends.

The apartment door opened into a sitting room containing two windows, one pointing westward and the other toward Don Boone's residence at the back. It contained a recently purchased chesterfield suite as well as a bookcase and a small coffee table and a dresser. In the middle was a place for a wood stove, as yet to be replaced.

From that sitting room were two bedrooms. Jim's was a long one and ran immediately along the right of the entrance door to the apartment. Ken's bedroom wall continued in line and encompassed two windows, one looking out the back toward Don Boone's and the other looking east toward Botwood. An opening in the partition between the bedrooms allowed light to enter Jim's room from the sitting-room windows. Jim's bedroom had no window to the outside. It was essentially a large closet.

The café level could be accessed from either side of the building right along Water Street. The building itself was situated so close to the road it made more sense from a safety perspective as cars passed perilously by. The main café component ran about forty-two feet long north to south by twenty-eight feet wide east to west.

The main counter was on the right-hand side near the east entrance, while the kitchen was located farther along to the end of that wall. Washrooms and a smaller counter could be accessed from the west entrance, and the stairs to the living quarters were located at the end of that westerly café wall.

Thirteen booths lined the café walls, and seven tables were spread around. Seating near the front was relatively well lit, while seating along the walls was dull and uninviting. A jukebox and pinball machines were located near the counter on the west wall and were often the cause of conflict, depending on whom the patrons were at any particular time. It was here in this setting Hearsey spent most of her workday.

She recalled how Jim was convinced that Ken was a slow learner at best and actually mentally ill. To treat one's father the way Ken treated Jim was unheard of. There must be something wrong with him, surely. So convinced was he of this that he even approached William Fong, William Thompson, and Dr. Twomey, separately, to have them apply their influence to have Ken committed as mentally incompetent. They declined to do so, of course, since they did not share Jim's view about Ken, not to mention that such an undertaking was Jim's responsibility, not theirs. Jim never did make the decision to bring Ken in for an assessment himself. Their arguing was unceasing and sometimes went on in front of other customers. Hearsey wondered what the findings might have been, had Jim acted.

In time, Jim approached William Fong and others, this time for loans to keep his business going, but they were not prepared to risk their own livelihoods and family responsibilities for someone who could find money for gambling but not manage his business affairs.

Jim rarely left the café now, only to do banking, so visitations were seldom reciprocated. For some reason he seemed fearful to leave the café. He did this once or twice a year and felt no need to go more often, as he had a huge 800-pound safe downstairs, near which lay a twelve-gauge shotgun. It was the worst-kept secret in town.

16

The next day, Tuesday, November 4, Hearsey showed up for work at 9:30 a.m. but found herself greeted by a locked building. That was strange. She banged on all three doors for Jim to let her in but got no response. With a quick glance around, she noticed that all the windows were barred and the blinds pulled down. Where there were no blinds, the windows were covered with ten-test, a type of wallboard. Usually Jim shuttered only the two front windows. It seemed very strange. She had never seen this before.

Just then, Mr. Buckley showed up. "Jim told me last night after you left that he was sick, so he decided to close up until he was feeling better. By the way, Mr. Adams stopped by earlier this morning and asked if Jim was up. I told him he wasn't, so he left for work. I guess he's still sick."

That was unusual for Jim, Hearsey thought, so she hung around until 10:30 a.m. Tired of waiting, she went home and called the café, but she received no answer. She waited a couple of hours and phoned again, and still there was no response.

Concerned, Hearsey decided to call Frank Adams at his store downtown. Had he heard anything?

"A couple of hours after you left yesterday, I dropped by the café. Mr. Buckley told me that Ken was planning on going to Grand Falls on the 6:30 bus," he informed her. "Oh, by the way, I saw smoke coming through the chimney earlier this morning but saw no sign of Jim."

Hearsey had checked. There was no smoke when she left. The fire must have gone out. She was becoming a bit unnerved. "How strange that he could light a fire and not be able to answer his phone or the door, or even call out."

After his store closed, Mr. Adams went back to the café. Standing outside Jim's bedroom on the ground, he called out, "Jim!"

He got a response. "Who this?" came Jim's feeble voice from inside.

"This is Frank, Jim. Are you sick? Do you need a doctor?"

Jim replied, "No, no, no," in a casual tone, certainly not angry, but rather fatigued, and then the building went very quiet.

Since he believed Jim, Frank, who had a heart condition, felt the right thing to do was to simply leave the man alone. He often felt the same way when he was not feeling well. Frank recalled the conversation around suppertime on Monday and naturally believed that Ken had gone to Grand Falls to the movies, so everything seemed fine enough, and he relaxed and went home. Perhaps Ken was lying down, too. He dismissed it from his mind, had supper, and retired early.

Early Wednesday morning, November 5, Guy Fawkes' Day, Linda was troubled because Hearsey was so upset about the Lings. "Come on, Hearsey, let's stop in to the Chinese stores and ask about Ken. Maybe they have heard something."

"Good idea," said Hearsey. Finishing breakfast, they first dropped over to Wong's, right alongside. Then it was up over the hill to Williams's Candy Store, and then down all the way to Northern Arm Stores. Hearsey told each of them of her fears for Ken's safety, but she emphasized that it was also possible that Jim was in danger. Their disagreements were so heated at times, and this barricading of the building and installation of barbed wire was too much to ignore. Through her efforts she hoped that the Chinese would react as a group and implore the police to investigate. Both she and Linda knew where they stood on the social ladder. They didn't even make it to the bottom rung, so who was going to pay any attention to them? But she figured they would listen to the Chinese as a group.

They hadn't seen or heard from Ken and didn't give Hearsey's concerns much weight. Being ignored was something the girls were used to.

"What's the matter with these people, Linda?" said Hearsey.

"It's heartbreaking. Can they not step forward? Sure, my

God, Aunt Hearsey, these people play cards with Jim. And all of a sudden they're ignoring him? What's that all about?" Linda spat in response. Linda was not often angry, but this time she had had it.

They had not considered the numerous incidents that had been visited upon the Chinese citizens over the years, resulting in a distancing on their part from the Lings. But what the Chinese did not know was the litany of issues and the resulting tension building between the two. Is was not an enviable position for the Canning ladies to find themselves in. But Hearsey was no quitter.

She would try once more, tomorrow, to get Harvey Fong to listen to her.

During lunch hour on Wednesday, Frank Adams walked over to the café and again tried to talk with Jim, but received only vague responses. He went on up to his home, had his lunch, and returned to his store. That evening he called Harvey Fong, asking if he had any news on Jim's condition.

Frank asked Harvey to go down to the café, but Harvey felt that Harry Chow from Windsor would have more success. He would get back to Frank.

Meanwhile, Mok Yeung, having had a visit from Hearsey and Linda Canning, came to Harvey Fong's house to report that he had attempted to get into the café, as he had heard from the ladies that Jim had gone into seclusion. He had tried to get in twice, with no success, and was concerned.

Harvey explained that he was aware of the situation and that Mok should put it out of his mind. He would be working with Harry Chow to resolve the situation.

Harvey Fong then called Harry at the Globe Restaurant to inform him that Jim had once again locked the doors to the café and refused to let anyone in or even talk with anyone. Harvey asked him to come to Botwood to see if he could reach Jim.

Harry Chow showed up that evening around 8:30 p.m. Mr. Chow knocked on the front doors and called out to Jim, clearly identifying himself. He called out three times. Three times he was met with silence. Next, he went to the side window, where he met Frank Adams, who had noticed the activity from his home. Frank told him that Jim was sick. Harry called out to Jim again, this time in Chinese, begging him to let him in.

Jim finally responded. "I in bed sick and don't want to get up."

Harry Chow then left and dropped down to Wong's to discuss the situation with Victor. From there he called Harvey Fong and advised him that Jim gave him "no satisfaction," and returned home to Windsor.

Hearsey's anxiety had become so acute, she shared her frustrations with her mother. No one seemed to grasp the sense of urgency that had consumed her. Being fair, she had witnessed more than enough to convince her that either was capable of injuring or killing the other. She knew more than anyone the high level of tension, now having reached explosive proportions, that existed between the Lings. Now neither had been seen since Monday, and Ken was supposed to have gone to a movie in Grand Falls that night. He had simply vanished.

Cecilia Canning became even more alarmed than Hearsey as she heard her daughter pour out the details of what she was dealing with. When she heard that neither Jim nor Ken were answering the phone, or keeping the fire lit in freezing temperatures, and had the back windows covered in barbed wire, she was astounded. Moreover, they were not opening the door, not talking to anyone through the windows, and no one in the Chinese community could find Ken. There was no mistake about it. The Mounties should be alerted to investigate. This situation was totally outrageous.

She sat in disbelief as her daughter told her of her efforts to have someone take the lead. Hearsey was, after all, just a minimum-wage worker who had no status in the community. Hearsey had walked miles since Tuesday and made countless calls to those whose voices mattered in a futile attempt to have someone, anyone, lift the heavy burden from her shoulders. Jim Ling's Caucasian friends and neighbours knew there was something very strange transpiring. All they had to do was look out their windows.

Cecelia wondered, did everyone think her daughter was a fool? Who else in the world would put themselves through that if they were not convinced that action should be taken? The young woman didn't want anyone arrested, for goodness' sake. Neither did she want to see Jim nor Ken injured, let alone killed. A reasonable explanation for Ken's sudden disappearance was not too much to expect, yet there was none.

Hearsey couldn't count the number of times she had heard customers comment, "One of these days something very serious is going to happen between those two." And right now all the ingredients were there to qualify as one of those days, and it scared her. It should have scared others.

That Wednesday, she chose not go to the café, but rather, at 9:00 a.m. she phoned the Harbourview from home and got no answer.

"Mom, this is ridiculous. Up until Monday I couldn't move without Jim on the phone calling me at 7:00 a.m. and even well after midnight to see if I'm safe, and now I can't get him to pick up the phone. Now that's not normal."

"You're right, my dear, something is wrong."

Hearsey waited until early afternoon and called Frank Adams at his store to express her concerns. She wanted his advice. "Should I call the police, sir?"

"Well, Hearsey, something has to be done. There is something definitely not right about this."

Meanwhile, bizarre rumours were circulating, what with Ken missing and Jim being unstable. Ken was dead, either murdered or drowned. The gossip mill was operating on full steam.

Unable to suppress her concerns any longer, at 6:00 p.m. she called the police. She hesitated to do so, but no one with standing in the community was stepping up and there was so much pointing to something very wrong. There was no answer. She called again, but still there was no answer, and she left a message with the answering service.

No sooner had she hung up when the phone rang. It was Frank Adams. "Harry Chow has been down from Windsor and tried to persuade Jim to open the café, without success. Jim told him he was sick."

Hearsey was relieved, and she called the police again to cancel her request for help. However, something still nagged at her. There was no sign of Ken, and that was peculiar.

Wednesday was Bonfire Night, and during the day, young people moved their stores of boxes, boughs, tires, and barrels into position for the big bonfires that evening. There were countless piles stacked in potato gardens all over Botwood, where at 6:00 p.m. they would all be set ablaze.

Young and old alike would soon gather around the fires as the flames leapt skyward. Songs would be sung and marshmallows and potatoes roasted all in the fashion as had been done for years and years. This event rarely got out of control, even when the fires burned late into the night. The sharp smell of the coals would linger well into the next day.

17

Thursday, November 6, Hearsey called the café again at 9:00 a.m., but as usual there was no response. At 3:30 p.m. she dropped by Mr. Frank Adams's store before heading up the road to the Spot Cash to buy some items for her mother. There was no smoke coming out of Jim's chimney. A bad sign.

Harvey Fong was in his store, and he came over to speak with her. After some pleasantries, Harvey said, "If you are talking to Jim, don't say too much, as he might be crazy. Just ask him where Ken is, and leave it at that." His past experiences with Jim now led him to believe he had become mentally ill, and he was concerned for Hearsey. The level of anxiety of everyone close to Jim was rising rapidly.

Hearsey agreed with Harvey's counsel and then left to walk home, which took her once again past the café. Noticing there was now some black smoke coming from the chimney, her spirits lifted. She stopped to bang on the doors and call out. Hearsey then went around back and called out from the rear, but again there was no reply. She remained there fifteen minutes, pondering what to do. It was the first time she had seen smoke coming out of the café since Monday, and the weather every day since then had been extremely chilly, wet and windy. *They must be perishing in there*, she thought. *But if he can light a fire, surely he can answer a phone.*

She gave up and moved on down the road to Frank Adams's store again. From there she called the café several times. It was futile. When Mr. Adams closed the store at 7:00 p.m., Hearsey and Linda, her niece, walked to his house. Then Mr. Adams pulled on his boots and warm coat, and the three of them dropped over alongside the café. They went to the kitchen window and called to Jim for a while, then went around back by the coal pound that bordered on Don Boone's property.

Hearsey asked Mr. Adams to do something for her. "Would you place the ladder against the building so I can get up onto the porch?" He complied and positioned the ladder, and Hearsey fearlessly began climbing up onto the roof.

At that very moment, Bill Butler and his fiancée, Dot Lidstone, drove by, with their friend Albert "Moann" Hemmeon in the back seat. They saw movement at the rear of the café and pulled in by Dr. Gerald Smith's place. They could see Frank Adams standing at the foot of the ladder.

Bill was the first to speak. "What in the name of heaven is Hearsey doing climbing up that ladder, Dot? I never saw her do that before."

"It beats me, b'y. I guess she's trying to talk to Jim. He's been sick here lately, you know, and no one's been able to get in touch with him."

"She's just concerned, I suppose," Bill commented.

"You know she watches over him and Ken like a hawk," Dot replied. "You know, I hear he hasn't been himself since Ken burned that young German fella with the fat. Anyway, let's mind our own business and leave them alone."

It was odd, but nothing alarming. Unfazed, Bill continued to drive down the road to Wong's for a snack, as they often did.

Hearsey climbed up the ladder, stepped out onto the roof of the back porch extension, and went to the window on the left. She had to be careful of the barbed wire. After twenty minutes of knocking on the window, she finally heard Jim speak from the inside. "Who is it?"

Hearsey replied with the Chinese name Jim had given her. "Boey. Come down and let me in, will you, Jim?"

"No! No! No!" Jim sounded quite agitated.

"Where is Ken?" she asked.

"Me not know," he replied, his voice rising in volume and sharpness.

"Is he in there with you?"

Jim replied, "No! No No!" This time he was even louder and quite emphatic.

"Do you need a doctor?" Nothing. The place fell silent.

There was no question about it. By this time, Jim was coming unglued. He had screamed in such a high pitch and volume, Hearsey figured he had gone savage with rage and frustration. Her questions to him seemed normal enough. What the hell was going on?

Hearsey tried to keep a conversation going, but Jim simply shut down. Only silence came from inside the building. She kept listening for Ken's voice, or anything that might indicate he was inside and well. Her body shook with fear. Still, Hearsey and Frank and Linda waited silently, trying to comprehend Jim's behaviour, along with the fact that there was no sign of Ken.

Slowly and quietly, with tears spilling down her face, a greatly disturbed Hearsey descended the ladder, stepped off, and stood frozen, baffled as to what to do next in that drizzly, cold, windy night.

Frank Adams, Hearsey, and Linda lingered around the café a while longer, listening hard. Soon Hearsey, having heard nothing further, suggested they all return to Mr. Adams's house. All three were very worried now, especially Mr. Adams. No one knew Jim as well as he did. He had visited the café every day and was Jim's best friend in the world. This was beyond normal. It was insane.

Frank decided he had had enough. Something had to be done. He picked up the phone and called Harvey Fong and filled him in on what had just happened. His frustration and concern were unmistakable. It took a lot, but Frank was finally pissed off.

Harvey said, "I will call Corner Brook and Grand Falls and get back to you." About an hour later, he called back. Nobody had seen Ken. He also checked the Chinese community in Botwood. The response was the same. Nobody had seen Ken lately, and he hadn't said he was leaving town to anyone except Edgar Buckley.

"Harvey, should we notify the police?" Frank asked.

"Harry Chow will be down tomorrow," was Harvey's response. Their spirits sank. With that, Frank and Hearsey reluctantly agreed to leave things until the next day. Some years earlier, it was Mr. Chow who had persuaded Jim to reopen his café after having closed it for a week. Harvey felt Mr. Chow had a much greater chance to break through to Jim than he did.

A few minutes later, Harvey called again. He had just spoken to Harry Chow again, who had once more called around the province. All reports were that Ken had not been seen.

A deeply worried Harry Chow felt that, after all this effort by him and Hearsey Canning, it was time to approach the police. Sadly, it seemed his old friend was no longer responsive to him. Further intervention on his part, he reluctantly concluded, would not be fruitful. Additionally and most concerning, the fact that Ken had not been seen or heard from anywhere in the province could not simply be dismissed as some "misunderstanding or miscommunication."

"Harvey, you must make sure to tell the police they have to be careful. Jim has a gun in the café."

Harvey ensured him this message would be clearly passed on. At around 10:30 p.m., Hearsey and Linda, noting Frank's exhaustion, left to walk home. They would be passing right by the police station and would stop there along the way. If that failed, Hearsey would make the report in the morning.

Around 8:00 p.m., down at the police station, Red Bowen and Terry Hoey were finishing up some paperwork and waiting for the time to make their rounds. They would be on their own this evening, as Healey was in Grand Falls attending a Rifle Association event. Healey was temporarily in charge of the Botwood detachment, as the regular officer was in Regina attending specialized classes.

Before going on the regular evening run around town, Hoey decided to write his old buddy, P. G. Ryan, back in Regina. Terry was unable to finish the letter, since Bowen rapped on the door and told him it was time to make a routine cruise around town. Because it was so miserable out, they decided to take their pea jackets in case they had to get out and check on something. In a matter of a few minutes, off they went.

Police station, Botwood. Courtesy of Botwood Heritage Society.

Hearsey and Linda walked down to the station, climbed the Water Street stairs to the second level, and knocked on the door of the RCMP private quarters. It was their intention to report the matter in detail, after which they would continue on down the road to home. The police would then have enough facts to begin an investigation. If they were not in, they would continue on home and try again in the morning.

At that very second, the police cruiser pulled in. It was now around 10:20 p.m. Behind the wheel was Red Bowen. Also inside was Constable Hoey. They were just passing by the station on the way toward Peterview when they saw the two young women on the landing.

Hoey rolled down the window. "Yes, ladies, can we help you?"

Hearsey breathed a huge sigh of relief. She was forthright and got right down to business. "Who is in charge?"

"Constable Healey," replied Red, "but he is in Grand Falls at a meeting."

Standing by the car, Hearsey and Linda quickly relayed their concerns to the officers. Hearsey shared how Jim had not called or answered the phone since Monday, something he would never do. He always stayed in touch with her, no matter what.

Linda recounted to the officers the events of the previous days, leading up to their visit to the police. "It kind of started on Monday afternoon, when I walked up to the café to meet Hearsey, who was getting off early. As she was about to go out the door, she heard the beginnings of a conversation between Jim and Ken, when Ken said, 'She not coming, she not coming!' That's when their discussion got loud and angry, but Hearsey kind of dismissed it as nothing out of the norm. She and everyone else knew Jim's wife was not coming because of Ken's letter, so this must have pertained to Ken's wife. She felt that Jim was in denial regarding Ken, and in spite of it all, he wanted Ken to stay and be part of his life. And she had told him so. Jim used to smile at Hearsey, kind of silly, like, and say nothing. This went on for a couple of days and concerned even Mr. Adams."

"Because the place was locked up and there was no sign of anybody," Hearsey interjected. "We stopped in on the people who knew the Lings, but no one was alarmed. What was going on behind the scenes, we didn't know about.

"Finally, later on tonight we received word from Harvey Fong to go to the police station and to make sure the police knew there was a gun in the café. That's when we walked down to the police station and you fellows pulled in."

Constable Bowen asked them to get in the cruiser. They got in, and Hearsey continued to fill them in, and Linda picked up where she left off. Hearsey poured everything out as they drove up to the café.

"Wait a second. I need to make some notes," said Constable Hoey, reaching to his left for his notebook and pen. He began to write furiously.

Hearsey reiterated, "Harvey Fong told me to report what

is going on in the café because it's so strange. He wants you to know that Jim has a gun and can sometimes be unpredictable. The local Chinese have checked everywhere in the province where Ken could have gone, but he is not there. They have tried to get in, but can't. I'm afraid they might have gotten in a fight and one of them is injured or dead. Ever since the fat incident in October, they appeared to be getting along a lot better. But for some reason they were having heated words, and both were ready to erupt when I left work on Monday, and no one has been able to get in since. Not only has no one seen or spoken to Ken since by phone or otherwise, their stove has been lit only twice since then, only for a short time in these cold conditions we've been having the past week. Ken seems to have disappeared. It's the strangest thing."

Red had in fact noticed that the place had been closed for a few days, but he had thought nothing about it. *People can close their stores if they wish. It really is no one's business*, he had thought to himself. However, these new revelations caused him to reconsider that position. At 10:30 p.m. they pulled into the eastern parking lot of the café.

Frank Adams called Harvey Fong to report that the police were now on site. Harvey, now frantic, called Corner Brook once again, looking for Ken. He was not there.

"God Almighty, Jim, what the hell is going on over there, my friend?" a very heartsick Frank Adams said out loud.

18

The four exited the cruiser and walked around the building to the back. Looking up, they could see that there was a light in Jim's bedroom. It was shining into the living-room section, through which they could see. Hearsey pointed to the ladder standing against the extension, still in the same spot where she had climbed up on the roof and spoken to Jim.

Constable Bowen said nothing. He climbed up the ladder and stepped off onto the porch roof. He noticed both windows at the back were covered by barbed wire, which to him seemed extraordinary. He went to the window on the right, which looked into the living room. He called out, "Jim! Jim!" There was no response.

"Go to the window on the left," Hearsey called from below.

Bowen shifted to the left window. It was closed, and something covered the window from inside, preventing him from seeing into the room.

Terry Hoey had pointed the beam of his flashlight on that window, and Bowen ordered, tersely, "Turn off the light."

Tapping on the window, Constable Bowen called out, "Jim, this is Red, the Mountie. Come down and let me in. Is Ken with you?" Again there was no reply.

Bowen's numerous visits to the café in the past had been pleasant. Jim was always friendly toward him, and the other officers as well, as far as he knew. More often than not, he would give Red a Coke or some other treat. Their relationship had been excellent. But now he was standing on the roof, outside in the rain and the darkness, with an unresponsive Jim Ling inside. Bowen figured this was most unusual indeed. He commenced calling out again, several times, identifying himself each time.

"Jim, where is Ken? Would you please come down, Jim? We would like to speak with you."

"No, no, no! Go away!"

With that, all conversation ceased. All remained quiet inside.

Bowen decided to climb down and try another approach. He went back to the eastern side and turned to Hoey. "Would you bring the ladder around here and place it to the second window from the end, please?" He pointed to the window in question.

"Right away, Officer," replied Hoey, retrieving the ladder and putting it in place.

"That window can be opened from the outside," Hearsey offered.

Bowen cautiously climbed up, and nearing the top, he pushed up on the window. Sure enough, it slid upwards six inches. He called out firmly, "Jim, come out. This is Constable Bowen, the one you call Red. I am the policeman who comes to help you when you are in trouble. Come out. There is nobody going to hurt you." He had taken pains to make certain that Jim knew who he was. He waited a minute for a response.

"Go 'way! Come back tomorrow."

Bowen then pushed the window high enough to stick his head in and continued to call out to Jim. Silence was his only response.

He found himself looking into a large, dimly lit storage room. Suddenly, he caught sight of a person crawling down the stairs right in front of a doorway. Reaching for his flashlight and holding it crosswise over his head, he turned it on. He was too late. The figure had disappeared. Bowen turned off his light. Waiting about five minutes, he saw the head of an individual who was now crawling upstairs. Quickly, he switched his light on again, just in time to see Jim duck around a corner, still crawling. The light inside the café went out, and Bowen switched off his flashlight, then turned it on again, right away. There was Jim, once again, this time peeping around a corner.

This exchange went on a number of times. Bowen realized that nothing was being accomplished. He decided to get down and pulled the window to, leaving it open just a little.

Bowen was halfway down the ladder when Hearsey shouted loudly, to ensure that both he and Terry Hoey could hear, "Be careful, Jim has a gun in the building." It occurred to her that Bowen, in spite of her warning, might try to enter the building if he went up again. She felt the reminder was in order. Harvey had stressed that the police were to be warned. Harry Chow was adamant about that.

When he stepped off onto the ground, Hearsey requested to try and speak to Jim again. Bowen refused, as this had now become a police matter. It was in their hands now. She had fulfilled her responsibility. But Hearsey persisted, until he conceded, and up she went. Linda watched in fear and amazement as her aunt Hearsey was about to reach the top. Hearsey raised the window wider and put her head inside.

"Jim, Jim, this is Hearsey. This is Boey. Come down, we want you," she said in a pleading tone.

Jim spoke up. "No, no, no, me don't know you!"

Hearsey climbed down.

She and Linda watched as a friend of Jim's, a neighbour named Lang Nichols, came along. Without asking, he climbed the ladder, all the while calling out, "Jim! Jim! It's Lang." There was no reply.

"You're not going in there, Lang!" said Bowen, very firmly. "Now get down out of it!" Bowen wasn't happy.

Clearly, Linda, both police officers, and Nichols all heard Hearsey roar at the top of her lungs, through cupped hands, "No, no, don't let him go in! Jim got a gun in there! How many times do I have to tell you? Be careful!" They would have to have been stone deaf not to hear her.

Nichols came back down, reluctantly. Jim was his good friend, after all, and he was concerned for his welfare. It was that simple. He believed he could persuade him to come out. He wasn't the least bit scared. Jim would never hurt Lang.

Bowen scampered back up and pulled the window down again, leaving it open just a few inches, and descended the ladder.

Considering his next move, Bowen said to no one in particular, loud enough for Hearsey to hear, "I can't break and enter these premises unless I have a warrant." He was recalling the protocols for these situations. Part of the training in Regina.

"Why would I go to get a warrant anyway, Hearsey?" he asked.

Flabbergasted by the question, Hearsey stated bluntly, "Because there is a Chinaman missing since Monday. That should be reason enough," she said, her voice raised in a scolding manner and in disbelief. Had he not heard a word she'd said, coming up in the cruiser? "Oh my gosh, nobody listens to me, Linda." She was invisible to everyone. They just totally disregarded what she said.

Next, Bowen led them around to the kitchen window, and they all called out again, but to no avail. Hearsey stood up on a nearby bank that allowed her to see over the kitchen windowsill, her head not far from Jim's windowless bedroom. She heard what she thought was a rustling from inside, as if someone was in bed and had turned over, maybe. Or as if a spring had made the noise. As if something was now being pulled across the floor. It had definitely come from Jim's bedroom.

They listened intently when things fell silent again. Red decided it was time to turn this matter over to someone with more authority.

The officers climbed aboard the cruiser, drove to the police station, and reached Constable Healey's wife by telephone. She told them he wished to meet with them in Bishop's Falls by Wood's Service Station. She would drive him there, and they would pick him up. With that, they were off to rendezvous with Healey twelve miles away. Meanwhile, Boone and Nichols went to their respective homes, and Hearsey and Linda were invited to Frank Adams's house to await their return. Frank was feeling tired and a little overcome by now and was concerned about his heart condition. He didn't need another heart attack.

The officers lost no time. Fifteen minutes later, Bowen and Hoey saw the lights of Healey's parked sedan. He was wearing civilian clothes. He transferred to their car to be brought up-to-date. As they sped along to Botwood, Bowen and Hoey filled him in on the strange circumstances of the evening. Fifteen minutes later, they were back. The cruiser immediately pulled in alongside the Harbourview Cafe, and the officers climbed out to proceed to the eastern side of the building, where Bowen had last positioned the ladder.

Frank Adams, Hearsey, and Linda spotted them returning and noted the time. It was 11:40 p.m. The ladies decided to go over, but Frank, exhausted, watched from his living-room window.

In his civilian clothes, Constable Healey proceeded up to the ladder, which remained where Bowen had left it. When he reached the partially opened window, he called out in an authoritative manner, "Jim, come here. I want to talk with you. This is the RCMP." He was commanding now, not requesting.

Jim grunted something unintelligible. The police believed he was upstairs and in the living quarters at the back of the building, but there was no light to be seen. The blind was down. It was as silent as a tomb. Healey remained there for a few moments, considering his options.

"Who has a flashlight?" he asked.

"Right here," said Bowen, passing it over. With that, Healey climbed all the way up the ladder. Upon reaching the top, he looked in through the window. It was now raised about six inches. He peered into the large storage room, and to the right he saw a partition that separated the room from the other side, where they believed Jim and possibly Ken were located. Jim's bedroom.

Healey called out, "Jim, we are the RCMP. Please come out for a moment and talk to us."

The only reply was, "What?" followed by a few words Healey could not understand.

Bowen, observing closely, had an uneasy feeling. He turned to Hoey and softly said, "If he goes in, I'm going with him."

"I'll be right behind you," replied Hoey.

"My God, Linda, that man is going inside. In spite of what I told them, he's going inside," said Hearsey.

Leaving his position on the ladder, Healey crawled through

the window. With that, Bowen and Hoey removed their pea jackets. Bowen handed his to Hearsey, and without receiving instruction from Healey, he prepared to follow him up the ladder and inside.

Hoey, seeing what was unfolding, removed his jacket as well. He could see Linda shivering in the misty, snowy rain. He walked over behind her, opened up the coat, and wrapped it around her back and shoulders, closing it around her neck.

Linda was stunned by his kind act. She gazed in astonishment at the handsome young officer. It was the first time in her seventeen years that a man had acknowledged her existence, and he did so naturally and with kindness.

She turned to Hearsey and whispered out of earshot, "Did you ever in your life see anyone as handsome, Hearsey? And he's so young!" She was smitten.

Constable Hoey, now partway up the ladder, looked down and said, "Hearsey, will you go to the back of the building and watch the rear window to see if Jim comes out that way?"

"Yes, sir," she replied. "Now, you fellows be careful in there," she cautioned again, "Jim has a gun." She watched as he scurried up the ladder and disappeared into the darkness along with Healey and Bowen.

Hearsey was prepared to do as Hoey instructed, when Ambrose Nichols and others returned to the scene and took over for her. This allowed her to return to the ladder leading into the display room. Anxiously, she looked up and waited, wondering what was coming next.

It was now midnight, and a new day was beginning.

19

Don Boone was in the process of surveying his yard, as there had been a rumour that someone was seen sneaking around outside. He reasoned that perhaps this was Jim, and since he and all the regulars knew Jim had a gun, he figured Jim might be preparing to leave the building, possibly to go up to his concrete block manufacturing plant. He might have been contemplating taking a hostage. It was anybody's guess.

On close examination, all he could see was a cow that was lying down in the yard, perhaps the one whose bell he had heard earlier in the evening.

Don glanced over toward the café just in time to see a light go on upstairs in the living quarters. Since all the young cops were now inside the building, he had no one to whom he could relay this information. He made a mad dash for the phone in his house and called the police station.

Meanwhile, events were unfolding inside. Healey walked across the room to where a doorway led into the living quarters. Bowen and Hoey were close behind.

He knocked on the door and called, "Jim?"

Jim responded, but his words were garbled and impossible to understand. Healey turned the knob and found the door to be unlocked. He applied some pressure. The door, which was hung to swing inward, moved a little. It opened a few inches before it brought up against an obstacle. It was dark, and he couldn't be sure, but it appeared to be the back of a chesterfield or large chair. He couldn't see anyone inside, so he closed the door again. He might very well have been able to force it open farther but decided against it. There was not the slightest sound coming from the room. It was eerie.

Healey called out again, "Jim, it's the police," and unexpectedly got a response.

"Police?" In a questioning manner.

"Yes, it's the police, Jim. Please open the door."

Healey was standing at the door frame on the right-hand side, while Constable Hoey was standing to his left, directly in front of the door and facing it.

In the meantime, Bowen passed them both, turned to his left, and began to slowly creep down the stairs to the restaurant level, shining his flashlight around, looking for Ken. It seemed possible he could be there, since he wasn't in Grand Falls or Corner Brook.

Reaching the bottom, Bowen gingerly guided his way along the western wall, his flashlight beam darting left and right. He paused as his eyes swept the lower area. He then commenced walking the perimeter of the room, starting at his right, the western wall, and completed a circuit around to the kitchen area. Quietly yet hurriedly, he checked the various rooms, including the washrooms, in search for the missing young man.

He dropped to his knees, checked the various booths, and looked among the clothing racks, but he found nothing. He approached the kitchen, where there was a large freezer and refrigerator. One story had Ken's body chopped into pieces and placed in the kitchen freezer. With trepidation, Bowen opened the door of the freezer and looked in. There were various cuts of red meat and fish, and other perishables, including ice cream and ice cubes. To his relief there was no body, human or otherwise, not even a cat.

So it was only rumours after all, he thought. Ken was probably upstairs right now in the living quarters. Satisfied, he walked to the bottom of the stairs and began to climb up to relay his findings to Constables Healey and Hoey.

The officers were still together on the upstairs landing. Hoey turned to Healey and suggested, "Let's break the door down."

Healey replied, "No." He was still convinced he could talk Jim out. Hoey backed away from the door.

Just as Bowen was reaching the landing, there was a deafening shot that resonated throughout the café, made louder by the acoustics of the building.

Bowen thought, *What the hell was that?* His first impression was that it was a revolver. He looked past Healey, to Constable Hoey, who was still standing there. A hole was cut in the door, about five feet from the floor.

Hoey then staggered backward toward Bowen. Healey's ears were ringing from the percussive sound, but he was able to hear Hoey when he spoke.

"Red, I'm shot, I'm shot!" Terry cried out in pain, shock, and absolute disbelief.

Bowen, just a step behind Hoey, reached forward, and Hoey fell back into his arms. He gently said, "Lay down, Terry," and helped lay him back on the floor. Bowen was slipping into shock, but somehow he shook it off. He raced back downstairs and quickly opened the doors on both sides of the café, then raced back up to where Hoey lay.

Outside, still standing by the ladder, Hearsey heard an officer cry out through the open window, "He's been shot! Someone get a doctor! Someone get a doctor!"

Hearsey released a blood-curdling scream. Wringing her hands in dismay, she cried out in the darkness, "Jesus Christ! Jim shot himself, Linda! He's after committing suicide. He's finally done it!" The two ran up to Frank's to relay the news.

Someone came to Adams's door a couple of minutes later, frantically calling to Hearsey.

"Hearsey, come back down to the café right away and turn on the lights in the bottom level!"

She raced back over to find that someone had found the light switches already and turned them on. She was just in time to see Bowen, Bill Butler, Ken Dean, and Ben Elliott carrying someone to the front of the café and placing him on a table. She recognized his face at once.

"Oh my God, oh my God, it's the little Mountie! Jim has

killed the little Mountie! Where's Linda? Linda!" she screeched, racing up through the garden and back to Frank's place, tears streaming down her cheeks.

"The young fellow? The one that passed me his jacket? How can that be? Sure, Jim was inside in the living area. Did he open the door and shoot? What a sin, what a sin, what a sin!" said a shocked Linda, joining her aunt in her sorrow and dismay. She then burst into tears, as did Frank.

Through her sobs, Hearsey said, "I wonder is Jim all right." As much a statement as a question.

20

Bowen quickly gathered his thoughts as his young mate lay dying. Someone had fired through the door and hit Hoey in the left side of his chest. His heart was pumping a stream of blood through the massive hole in his chest. There was no way to contain it.

He had heard Healey order, "Get a doctor. Get a doctor now!" The commanding officer stayed on the top level.

Bowen looked down at Hoey again in dismay, then raced to the front door. He shouted to a familiar figure. "Get a doctor right away. Hurry!" One person was already running up through Frank Adams's yard, heading for Dr. Gerald Smith's house beyond.

The man burst into the café, hollering, "I'll go. Leave that with me. I'll get Twomey."

It was Vic Grignon, a hockey player with the Grand Falls ANDCOs team, who then jumped into his Hilltop Cleaners dry cleaning van, along with a friend. They sped down to Dr. Hugh Twomey's house, several hundred yards down the road. As they pounded on the doctor's door, Hearsey and Linda were inside Adams's house, on the telephone with the hospital. They were told that plasma and emergency supplies were on the way and staff were being prepared for what was coming.

Back inside the café, Bowen continued to try to comfort Constable Hoey as he lay in distress on the table. Red believed that Terry was dead. His chest was blown wide open, and the pocket that moments ago had held his notebook was missing from the impact of the blast. It was an outright disaster. *God help us!*

It was ten minutes after midnight. Locals, drawn by the action, began to congregate inside of the café to be of assistance in any way, forgetting that they, too, were in grave danger. Once they realized their peril, they sought cover inside, away from the stairwell, fearing that to exit was even more dangerous: Jim had full coverage and range from his living quarters upstairs.

Fifteen minutes after midnight, Dr. Twomey's wife, Mary, was on her way upstairs to go to bed when she heard a commotion outside. She saw two men running up to her door and calling out, "Get Dr. Twomey! This is an emergency!"

They came into the house and loudly and hysterically explained that a man had been shot in the Harbourview Cafe. It was absolutely urgent that the doctor get there at once.

Mary ran to the foot of the stairway. "Hugh, there's an emergency up at Jim the Chinaman's place. You're needed right away," she shouted.

In a flash, Dr. Twomey was down the stairs, grabbed his medical bag, and was out the door.

To Mary Twomey, it seemed like only seconds had passed from the time she shouted to him to seeing her husband go down the hill in his car. She went in her bedroom, which faced Water Street. She could see the eastern side of the café and the two back windows. She saw the car stop at the café and watched her husband go in. Mary figured there must have been a fight or some other kind of common situation. It was curious, though. The building was completely black, except for one light upstairs. A crowd was beginning to gather, and there was a lot of disturbance and raised voices. Next, she spotted a hospital employee she recognized as Mr. Sheppard, heading up the road past her house in his station wagon. A truck soon appeared as well, and they both pulled in alongside the eastern side of the café.

Dr. Twomey entered the café around 12:20 a.m. and surveyed the grisly scene. With the aid of a flashlight, he saw Constable Hoey lying on a table. An examination soon revealed that there was a gunshot wound in the left breast, below his left nipple. He watched as Hoey exhaled once, and stopped breathing. It was that quick, so severe was the wound. He immediately sent for Dr. Gerald Smith, who lived up on the hill, just behind

Frank Adams's house. Dr. Smith showed up in what seemed like a couple of minutes. Sadly, the plasma and other medical supplies just brought from the hospital were of no use. The young man was dead. History had been made. A horrible history, at that. Something no one wanted. Not even Jim Ling.

Moments before, Don Boone had been on the phone with the RCMP receptionist, when his wife, Sadie, raced in, crying out, "Don! Don! The children and I just heard a gunshot. What in God's name is going on?"

Don dropped the phone and made for the door. He bolted to the café, and through the open western door he saw the young Mountie he had been speaking with a little earlier. He was lying on a table and being attended to by someone, who was removing his boots. He could see it was Dr. Twomey, now busily engaged, attempting to save the young man's life. Don was shocked to overhear the doctor's pronouncement of the young man's death.

With this chilling development, Don turned and ran back up to the house, his face reflecting the horror he had just witnessed. He stumbled in and called out, "My God, Sadie! Jim just shot that young cop from Peterborough. Get the children and stop for nothing. We are going to Mom Boone's. No one knows what he'll do next." They all dashed out the back door, running in full flight, running for their lives. The trauma of that night would be forever burned in their memories.

Their quick exit was followed by the evacuation of the occupants of several houses adjacent to the Boone and Nichols families. It was mass confusion. The entire neighbourhood was in a state of bedlam, a strange mix of fear and wonder.

Art and Mrs. Thompson had just left the Legion and were down at Ben Elliott's house, dropping off Jean at her home. While there, Ben burst through the door. He had been working late in Grand Falls. "Jean! There's a racket going on up at the café. Jim just shot a Mountie. Where's my gun?"

"You lent it to one of your friends to go moose hunting, remember?" she replied.

DEATH AT THE HARBOURVIEW CAFE

"My God, so I did. Let's get up there, Art," he said, and in an instant Ben and Art were headed up the road toward the café. Dr. Smith, who has been sitting with a couple of civilians alongside the café in a former police cruiser, spotted Ben. He left the cruiser, carrying his pump-action shotgun, and confronted Ben. He insisted he take the gun, just in case. Ben took the shotgun and stepped inside, while Art hurried over to Ambrose and Winnie Ball's property where a group had already gathered to begin preparing food. Throngs of men were now gathering and milling around.

It was going to be a long night.

Shortly before midnight, the phone rang unexpectedly at Hugo Thulgreen's house, located near Wong's Restaurant. It was the RCMP receptionist, who told him he was needed at once at the Harbourview Cafe. He hauled his clothes on and raced to the scene. Hugo was a member of the RCMP auxiliary force.

He was fully alert as he pulled in by the café. Gazing through the eastern door, he could see that Constable Bowen was being assisted in bringing Terry Hoey down to the lower level by Ken Dean, Bill Butler, and Ben Elliott. Ken and Ben were members of the St. John Ambulance, and Bill was involved with the fire department.

Hugo had overheard Dr. Smith, as he passed a pump-action shotgun to Ben Elliott at the doorway, saying, "Ben, you can't go in there without a gun. It's simply too dangerous. Here, take this. It has four rounds and is ready to use." It seemed like good advice to him.

Ben went inside, and once there he was immediately drawn into the events that had happened. He watched as Dr. Twomey attended Hoey's grievous wound. Hugo saw the young fellow's chest blasted wide open, giving an unobstructed view of his heart, still beating while his life's blood spilled out onto the table. Within a couple of minutes, Dr. Twomey made the dreaded death pronouncement, to no one's surprise, the wound being so substantial.

Around 11:45 p.m. the Seaport Orchestra had just concluded a practice on Wireless Road, and Kenneth Dean was headed back home in his stake-body truck, which on many occasions, in the absence of an ambulance or hearse in town, was used to fill their functions. As Dean was approaching the café, he noticed lots of cars and people there, so he decided to check it out. He was immediately called upon to transport the young Mountie's remains.

Dr. Twomey and a couple of citizens got in the back of Dean's truck, where Hoey now lay, and they sped off in the direction of the morgue. The morgue was located in a separate building behind the hospital, in what was once the Quartermaster's Stores during the war. Its facilities made it suitable as a morgue.

Before leaving the café, Dr. Twomey instructed those remaining to construct a barricade by the main counter, in the event that Jim should come downstairs shooting. This was a real possibility. That left Ben Elliott with the only firearm to fend off an attack.

21

Ensuring that nothing would be moved or misplaced or contaminated in any way in his absence, Dr. Twomey prepared to leave the hospital to return to the scene of devastation. In no uncertain terms, he left strict instructions with the staff before he raced out the door. He realized that official investigations would follow in days to come. Nothing was to be touched until he returned. After attending to matters at the hospital, Dr. Twomey would return to stay the night at the café. Ken and Hugo would also stay the night in case they were needed. No one could predict how this night would play out.

Meanwhile, Healey, the commanding officer, had turned his attention to the matter at hand. It was obvious to all that the situation for the Mounties was dire. There were only two of them left, and they had no weapons with which to deal with this potentially deadly situation. Still upstairs, he went across the display room to the ladder again and descended. He hailed a car at the scene to transport him back to the police station, where he immediately called Grand Falls and explained the nightmare that they were in. Requesting an immediate response from all available personnel, he then went to the strongbox and retrieved his revolver, fully aware that Bowen and others back at the café were in mortal danger. With that, he hurried back to the scene.

In his absence, Bill Butler quickly appraised the situation. Decisions needed to be made, and fast. *Those poor young bastards are caught with only riding crops on which to rely. That's less than useless should Jim choose to run down the stairs firing his twelve-gauge.* Those young fellows certainly did need help, he thought to himself. Then and there, Bill decided they were going to get it. He climbed into his vehicle and headed back up toward Wireless Road and King's Ridge Road. He knew the hunters who lived there, and he woke them up, starting with Norm Gill. He shouted to Norm, "Bring out your guns right away. Hurry! The Mounties are in trouble and need help." As he received the guns in the doorways, he requested they call others to have their guns ready for a quick pickup. It was November, and since the hunting season had commenced in October, locating rifles and shotguns would be no problem. In no time he had gathered what he believed was an adequate supply, and he headed back to the café.

Upon re-entering the café, it occurred to Dr. Twomey that he might be able to get a positive response from Jim. Jim had been a patient of his for years and was very well-known to him. It was worth a try. Dr. Twomey began shouting to Jim and kept it up for ten minutes. He made a concerted effort to ensure that he identified himself each time. He even offered Jim the opportunity to surrender, personally guaranteeing his safety. There was no reply. Just silence. The doctor paused a while to collect his thoughts before repeating the offer. Again, only silence came from Jim's quarters.

By now, Dr. Twomey realized it was a wasted effort. The only thing he could do at this point was remain in the café to tend to any other possible victims. A dejected Twomey had done his very best to defuse the situation. There was nothing more to do but wait.

Bill Butler arrived back at the doorway on the western side just as Healey came through the opposite door. Civilians were now inside the café, milling about, oblivious to their peril. Dr. Twomey called Healey aside and confirmed the worst. Hoey was deceased.

Healey shivered. His blood ran cold. He turned toward Bowen and said, "Red, go to the station right now and get your revolver. While you're there, call Grand Falls and update them on what has happened here. We need them to order a tear gas detail from Corner Brook straightaway. We urgently require backup down here. Make sure and tell them to bring floodlights and to move it. Anything can happen now at any minute."

1st. Floor

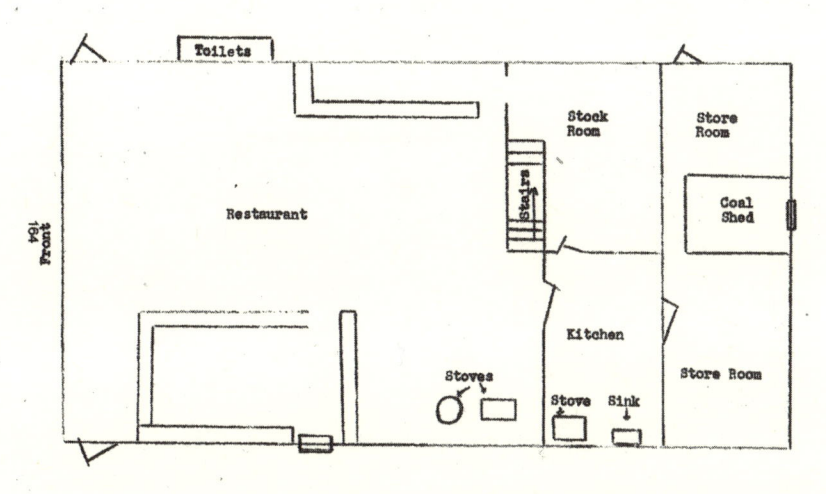

Layout of downstairs of the Harbourview Cafe. RCMP diagram.

Red rushed off toward the detachment office to carry out his instructions. He picked up the phone and placed the call. Everyone would soon be in the loop. He retrieved his revolver and returned to the scene at once. Shaken, he now realized that when he saw Jim sneak downstairs and back up again, it was in fact to get the shotgun that was in the building. Its location was a detail he had not been aware of, although it was common knowledge in the community rumour mill.

Upon his return, Healey was surprised when Bill Butler came through the opposite door, this time carrying a supply of guns. "Officer," said Bill, "I know you fellows had no firepower here, so I took it upon myself to gather these guns from the local hunters." With that, he passed them over.

An appreciative Healey thanked him and proceeded to distribute the weapons. For everyone to hear, he said, "These will be taken to the station after this matter is settled. From there, their owners can claim them."

Healey raised his voice in a commanding tone. "Now listen up. Nobody does any shooting without instructions from me. We want to take Jim and Ken into custody, not kill them. This

FRED HUMBER

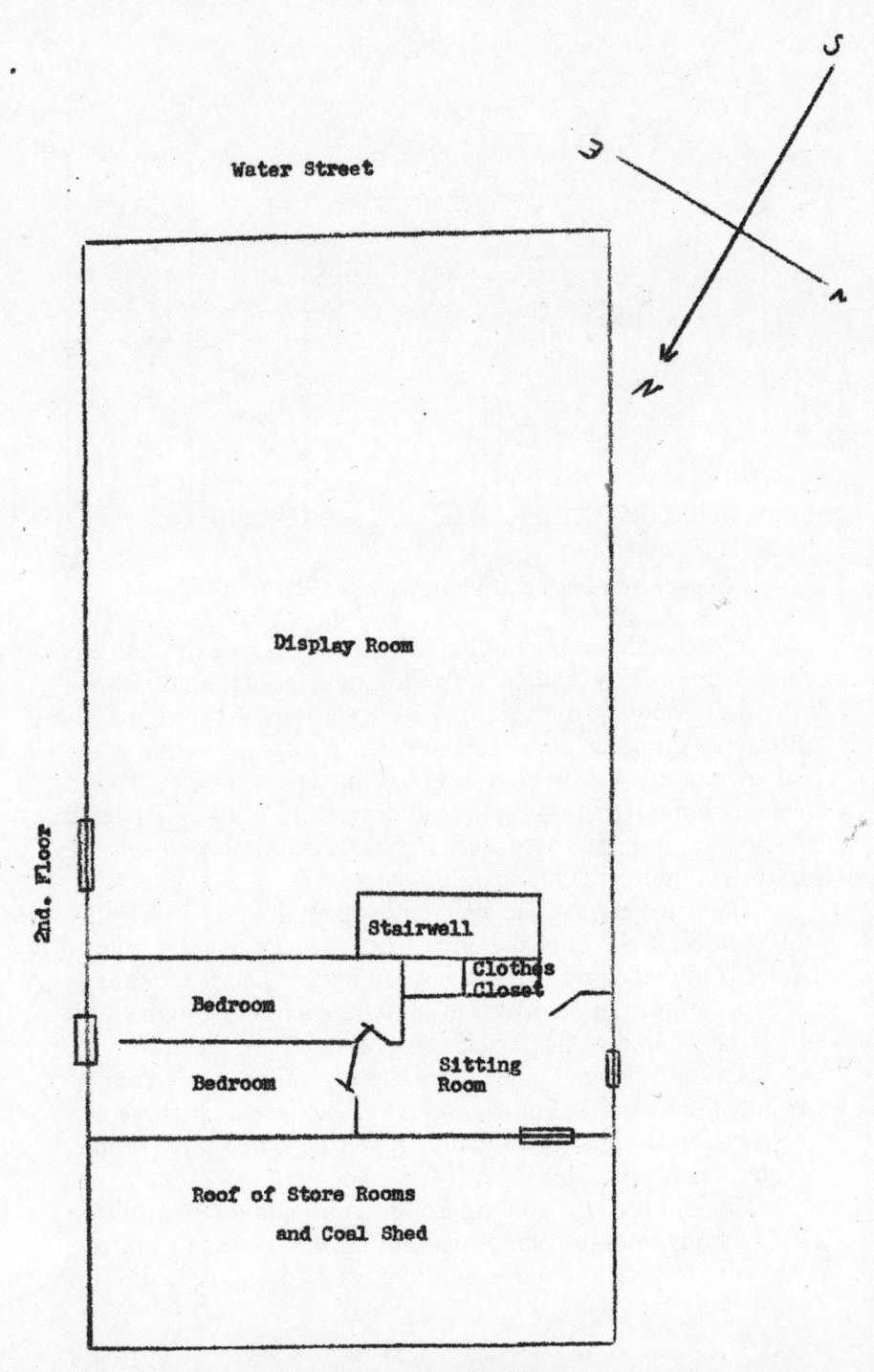

Layout of café upstairs and downstairs. RCMP diagram.

situation is uncertain, so keep out of range and under cover, and don't bunch up."

Civilians were then strategically placed around the perimeter of the building, and cars were positioned so their headlights could give maximum illumination. There were still townspeople inside, hiding behind counters and tables. The fear remained that Jim might try to escape and take hostages. No one could know anything for certain, but Constable Healey was taking no chances.

Thirty-five minutes after midnight, Corporal Hubert Taylor, resting at home in Grand Falls, received a call from Corporal Foster. "Constable Healey just advised me that Terry Hoey has been shot. Drop everything and get over to the detachment office." Taylor and Foster both scrambled to the office and began to call in various off-duty officers. Yet another call came in, this one from Red Bowen, with the devastating news that Hoey had just passed away.

Meanwhile, Foster was on the phone with Inspector Argent in Corner Brook, relaying the update. Things were moving quickly, as this was now a major crisis needing an appropriate response of speed, manpower, and equipment. The message relayed to Argent suggested it was likely that a tear-gas response would be needed to drive the shooter from his quarters. Argent quickly absorbed the information and paused to focus on the shocking drama unfolding.

"Foster, I am assembling a gas team immediately," he replied. "As soon as men and equipment are at the ready, we will be on the way. Road conditions being the way they are, we should arrive there somewhere around 7:30 a.m. Meantime, the situation is in your control. Emotions run high in crises, Corporal. Lives are at risk. Stay focused on your training and things will work out. See you soon." With that, Foster heard a click in the receiver.

22

In Grand Falls, they focused on matters unfolding in their own office. As the officers streamed in, they received their orders. "Listen up. We've lost an officer tonight. Pay attention! Go to the strongbox and retrieve your revolvers. Then get back here as quickly as you can."

They returned in less than three minutes. "We are going into a tricky situation. Get rid of any crap you have going on in your heads. Your life and the lives of others may depend on it. We may be dealing with a mental case when we get to the scene. Gentlemen, remember your training. Procedure! Procedure! Procedure! As you were taught in Regina. We have two officers, Healey and Bowen, who are under extreme pressure and are awaiting our arrival. How many are here?"

"Eight," someone replied.

"Good. Let's go, men. Be careful down there. And watch out for Fancy's Turn. You know how bloody dangerous that can be, especially this time of night. Corner Brook is on the way and will arrive around 7:30 a.m. That means that right now we have responsibility for what happens down there. Let's go."

With that, they streamed out and climbed aboard their cruisers. Twenty minutes later, they pulled in alongside the café to a much appreciative Healey and Bowen.

In short order the Corner Brook Gas Response Team gathered the necessary equipment and were on the way, over the long, treacherous gravel road that would in several hours place them at the scene of this dangerous and unexpected situation. Inspector Argent was shocked by the fact that only a few days before he had welcomed young Terry Hoey to Corner Brook, laughed with him, showed him around, and then saw him off to his first placement, the uneventful port of Botwood.

A relieved Healey left the café to greet Corporal Foster and the Grand Falls detachment, whereupon he relinquished command.

Foster was hastily brought up to speed, immediately took control, and sprang into action. On their arrival they noticed that numerous civilian vehicles were strategically placed with their headlights directed at the building. Also, floodlights had been secured from the A.N.D. Company and set up around the building, positioned to keep the entire café under surveillance. An armed guard comprised of RCMP and volunteer local citizens had been set up surrounding the building to prevent a breakout.

Foster now instructed that civilians turn in their weapons, as the reinforcements were sufficient to deal with the crisis.

"Set up roadblocks on both sides of the café," Foster commanded his officers. In a matter of moments, civilian cars were moved back out of range and roadblocks put in place. The last thing he wanted was for someone else to be killed or injured.

He recognized that the assistance from these local people had been crucial under the circumstances and was very much appreciated. The roadblocks, while necessary, resulted in traffic coming to a complete standstill from both directions, except for Circular Road, which veered away from the scene of hostilities. This posed some inconvenience but was absolutely essential for the safety of all concerned.

Around 3:00 a.m. Foster was told that some latecomers, armed civilians, had arrived. They were enraged by the death of Hoey and wanted to charge the building to neutralize Jim Ling.

They soon departed the scene and left for their homes, but only after Foster sternly stated that their guns would be seized if they didn't leave.

Around 12:30 a.m., as events were unfolding, Ted Mills and Fred Budgell, both eighteen years old, were just returning from Grand Falls after visiting girlfriends. As they approached the café on the main drag in Russ Mercer's taxi, which they had hired for the night, they found the road sealed off, forcing them to park in the public parking lot across from the A.N.D. Company wharf offices. Police cruisers and cars were everywhere, and people were coming and going.

"What the hell is going on, Ted?" Fred asked. Ted was about to ask him the same thing.

Curiosity prevailed, and they both got out of the car and walked up through the freezing rain, sleet, and wind to the scene of the chaos, unaware they were in mortal danger of dying from a bullet from Jim, who was barricaded inside, upstairs in the living quarters. At the entrance they were grabbed by someone and pulled inside, out of danger. Thus they entered the café, uninvited and unchallenged.

There was a crowd inside consisting of firemen, citizens, and police. Among others, they recognized Ben Elliott and Bill Butler.

They heard Ben Elliott being greeted outside by Dr. Smith at the opposite entrance, who cautioned him about the potential danger and extended a shotgun in his direction. Ben accepted the gun, which turned out to be the only civilian gun in the building apart from Jim's. Constable Bowen instructed Ben to cover the stairs as he and Dr. Twomey focused on other matters inside.

Ben Elliott attempted to reassure and calm Jim. He had often done business with him. "This is Ben Elliott, Jim," he called out in his loud voice. "Will you come down and give me a Coke?" There was no response.

He then added, "Don't forget, now, Jim, that I want to buy some concrete blocks. You know, the ones we discussed several weeks ago? I want to place the order now. I have the money here to pay for it in advance. Can you come down?"

There was still no response. Something briefly made a noise upstairs, like something falling down or tipped over, but the place fell quiet again. Ben reacted and ran to the bottom of the stairs, gun in hand, and attempted to go up the stairwell.

Upset, Healey shouted, "Ben, don't go up there!" Healey was not happy, and Ben knew it.

Hearing another loud sound upstairs, someone cried out, "Take cover!" Everyone complied, moving over on the eastern wall, in a corner away from the stairs. Once again, silence settled over the café.

Ben asked Healey, "Should we fire if Jim comes out?"

The officer replied, "Only if he comes out shooting. Otherwise, if he is unarmed, absolutely not."

To reinforce his reply to Elliott, Officer Healey instructed the other volunteers not to go up the stairway and not to shoot at Jim unless he came at them firing. Further, they were to cover the stairway from behind the counter. Once things settled down, Ben was asked to remain at the scene in case the officers needed assistance, until help arrived from Corner Brook later in the morning.

A large mirror was removed from the western wall and positioned at the foot of the stairs, to reflect up toward the landing at the top of the stairs and detect movement.

Around 2:00 a.m. an officer was sent to Harvey Fong's house to request his help in persuading Jim to surrender. Past experience had convinced Harvey that he did not have the kind of relationship with Jim that would be of help. Further, he felt that Jim was mentally ill, and the only one who had any hope of dialogue was Harry Chow. Hence, he elected to stay at home with his family.

Around 3:00 a.m. Corporal Taylor heard shuffling, like someone dragging something across the floor upstairs. That seemed odd. Then all was quiet. He and Bowen settled back to await the arrival of Inspector Argent and his team from Corner Brook. He would call out to Jim yet again during the night, identifying himself and telling Jim what he had done, in an effort to get him to give up, but there was no response.

Dr. Twomey, ever observant, noticed Bowen struggling with his emotions. Calling both him and Healey aside, he commented, "I believe you would be well served if you took some time off now and went home to get a little rest. That is my opinion as a doctor." Healey got the message and nodded his approval. With that, Bowen reluctantly left the café. He would return a few hours later, unable to close his eyes, and feeling the need to be available if required.

Throughout the night, Healey repeatedly attempted to communicate with Jim, but all to no avail. Things eventually settled down. The teenagers, Fred Budgell and Ted Mills, spent the night there, more frightened than they had ever been in their lives. The temperature outside was cold, and inside there was no source of heat. The teens were chilled to the bone, as they were not dressed for a night spent in an unheated building. At daybreak, they were ordered outside by an RCMP officer and Ben Elliott. Ray Dean and Ben Elliott had been asked to remain at the scene until reinforcements arrived from Grand Falls, but they had chosen to stay on much longer, until morning.

At approximately 7:30 a.m. Inspector Argent and his team arrived from Corner Brook, whereupon he took command. Discussions began with Corporal Foster and Constables Healey and Bowen as to the best way to approach the problem. Considerable deliberation followed, leaning heavily on Red Bowen's firsthand knowledge of the café. Argent wanted to know for certain if there were any children in the living quarters and just how many people were inside. Assured there were none confirmed other than Jim, Argent decided that they should assume that, if Ken was in there, he was under considerable duress.

Constables Bowen and Crowe and Corporal Taylor were now inside, guarding the stairway leading to the top floor, in case Jim should suddenly appear. Discussions continued regarding the layout of the building, following which Argent made a decision. The Inspector was quite cognizant of the danger involved in dislodging Jim, and in the interests of all concerned, he had weighed the facts carefully. He resolved to use tear gas to dislodge Jim and end the crisis.

23

Graham LeDrew, the fire chief, was called away from his work station at the company shed. At the café, Constable Gillingham explained the situation to him. LeDrew, a highly respected leader in the community because of his intellect, his volunteerism, and his generous nature, was astounded by what had happened overnight. His friend had killed an RCMP officer and was barricaded inside his café. Graham and Jim were "thick as thieves" and thoroughly enjoyed each other's company and discussions. All that aside, Graham immediately recognized the gravity of the situation and focused on the possibilities. To have Jim taken into custody unharmed was everybody's goal. Argent informed him it was very unlikely that a fire would break out. He had never heard of such a case in his twenty-five years on the RCMP gas team. But just in case, he insisted that preparations be made. Hearing this, the fire chief immediately ordered his crew and volunteers to prepare and lay out firehoses from the pumping station alongside. Meanwhile, Argent and Fitzpatrick were putting things in place for the raid.

Inside, Sergeant Fitzpatrick instructed Officer Taylor in the use of tear-gas grenades. These were to be used in conjunction with tear-gas canisters to be fired from a riot gun into the living quarters on the eastern side. This job was to be handled by Staff Sergeant Fitzpatrick, assisted by Argent. Taylor and the others were to remain inside the café.

Upon hearing the first canister fired, Taylor was to race up the stairs and throw a grenade in front of the living quarters. Then he was to quickly throw another over the stairway to the end of the display room. With this strategy, they hoped to take

Jim into protective custody and thus achieve a quick and peaceful resolution to the standoff.

Meanwhile, Ben Elliott had arranged to obtain John Evans's mail truck and drive it up into Frank Adams's uphill-sloping driveway, immediately to the east of the café. He stopped near the end of the building, just fifty feet across from the rear window. As well as protection, the truck offered an excellent position from which to launch the canisters.

With that, Elliott exited and crouched, making his way to high ground to the left of Frank's house and into the trees. There, unexpectedly, he came upon Dr. Craig, who was taking cover in the midst of the confusion. Ben continued on past the rear of the building and found himself looking down upon the scene. He could clearly see Constable Gillingham, Fire Chief LeDrew, and Junior Locke laying out water hoses.

Mary Twomey was standing outdoors. She noted that things remained uneventful until around 8:30 a.m., when Jack Evans's white mail truck driven by Ben Elliott passed by her house. That was unusual.

It pulled up alongside the café, on the eastern side, into Adams's driveway, and the driver got out of the truck. He started climbing the hill in the direction of Frank Adams's house. Two officers ran from the building toward the truck, one carrying a long-barrel gun. She would learn later it was Staff Sergeant Fitzpatrick. The other checked the windows at the end of the café. Fixated, she watched as the gun was raised. Seconds later, a shot rang out. A canister went flying in through the top pane of the window on the end of the cafe. It seemed to lodge in the ceiling. Immediately, a puff of smoke appeared inside, which then poured out through the window and dropped down onto the ground. It was obvious to her that it was tear gas.

The officer raised the gun a second time and fired. However, this time his shot went through the lower pane, and it seemed to catch in the curtains. There was a brief pause, and suddenly a burst of flame shot out that same window. But there was no smoke! The tongue of flame burst through the eastern window

DEATH AT THE HARBOURVIEW CAFE

and quickly spread up the side of the building, licking its way toward the roof shingles.

Crowe, Bowen, and Taylor were inside the café, in the lower level near the stairway. They were now wearing gas goggles and mouth protectors, awaiting the signal. The instant Taylor heard a shot fired, he ran up the stairs and threw a hand grenade onto the top landing, directly in front of the entrance to the living quarters. It fell alongside the door. The hole in the door loomed large. He raced back down the stairs, grabbed a second grenade, ran back up, and threw it toward the window by which the Botwood officers had entered around midnight. The entire top level was quickly enveloped with gas.

Armed standoff, November 7, 1958. Photo by Leo Dominic. Courtesy of Elmo Waterman and Marie Byrne Watkins.

At once, smoke belched from the grenades and began to flow down over the stairs. They heard the riot gun explode once again.

Someone outside had spotted Jim. He was pointing a gun. "Hit the dirt! Hit the dirt!" came a loud voice. A second later, shots were heard from upstairs.

Even though this had been anticipated, the shots were loud and jolted Taylor. Adrenalin rushed through his veins as he was gripped by an overwhelming sense of fear.

He ran toward the eastern door while Crowe and Bowen remained inside, calling out to Jim and pleading with him to surrender. They repeated this several times, but without success. Meanwhile, tear gas continued to roll downstairs into the restaurant area, making it difficult to see and forcing them both to move back. Again they heard shots fired, but they couldn't pinpoint their origin. A voice from outside yelled, "Fire! Fire! The place is on fire!"

With that, Bowen bolted from the lower level to the outside through the western door, as Crowe took one last quick look up the stairwell, and yet again called out to Jim to surrender. It was to no avail. He followed Bowen outside. He was the last to leave the building.

Aided by the blustery wind, the smoke drifted and rolled along the street toward the Twomey house, and Mary began to inhale the acrid chemicals. This made her stomach sick, and she wanted to throw up. By now the house was completely surrounded by smoke, and she could no longer see, her eyes watering so profusely.

"Oh, Hugh, Hugh, are you all right?" she cried out. Her terror was genuine and well founded. She turned to make her way into the house, finding herself overwhelmed by the chemicals. Mary hoped that her husband would return soon.

Judy Burry Noseworthy recalls, "The café burst into flames and the wind was quite breezy. The word was that there was danger of it following a path down Water Street, where it could hit the Adams house, the town office, Twomey's, the schools, and even the hospital. It was terrifying. Poor Dr. Twomey was driven mad trying to control so many things, especially Mr. LeDrew's situation. Knowing the fire was descending toward his home, he asked us girls if we could get some boxes together and go up to evacuate Mel and the two children, as she was all alone. We ensured everything was safe in the hospital and prepared boxes for the potential evacuation of the Twomeys'. But before long, word came that the fire had been brought under control with help from firefighters from surrounding communities. With that, we went back to our regular duties."

Dr. Twomey left the hospital and headed home, concerned about his wife and family. Suddenly, shots were ringing out from the café but from which side, Mary Twomey couldn't be sure. Fumes and smoke had drifted down Water Street and completely engulfed her home. She was uncertain as to what to do. Her door swung open to reveal her husband and their friend, Tom Antle. What a relief! Against Mary's wishes, Dr. Twomey, alarmed by the turn of events, insisted that she leave with Antle and accompany him to his home near the tarmac by the base, a much safer location, farther away from the action. His duty as a doctor lay with those at the scene of devastation.

On the western side across from the café, Graham LeDrew, still running hose and protected by a large truck, had spotted flames suddenly coming from upstairs. *Jim is going to die if we don't get this knocked down*, he realized.

There was no hesitation. Jim Ling, this beautiful, kind-hearted man from China, his friend for many years, was in mortal danger. LeDrew left the protection of the vehicle and leaped into action. Throwing all caution aside, he grabbed a hose, assisted by Junior Locke.

LeDrew made a turn to his left, intending to run up the ladder to direct a spray of water into the upstairs. A shot rang out, hitting him and taking a large part of his right arm at the elbow. Flesh, bone, blood, and number 12 shot were sent flying in the direction of Don Boone's house. Graham screamed, his arm dangling. "Oh, my arm, my arm! Help me!" He fell, twisting and turning in agony.

A second shot rang out, and this time it was Locke's turn.

He dropped to ground, grazed in the leg. Volunteers tried to drag both LeDrew and Locke out of firing range, to an adjacent house owned by Ambrose Nichols. Dr. Twomey tried to get to them, but he risked death to do so.

Constable Lloyd Saunders raced flat out to the nearby houses, pounding on doors, shouting orders to the residents to move to the rear of their homes. Lead was flying everywhere, striking Don Boone's house and Am Ball's garage. Death was one bullet away. Thankfully, responding to calls for assistance, fire departments were now responding from Grand Falls and Bishop's Falls and were due to arrive in about ten minutes.

Meanwhile, Ben Elliott crawled on his hands and knees around the back and to the western side, looking for a doctor for the wounded. He spotted Twomey on the far end of the building. The doctor was waiting on the corner of the café, trying to get to the wounded. He couldn't make it. It was too dangerous. By this time others had joined in the rescue attempt, pulling the injured men toward protective cover.

Out of nowhere came a cry of alarm. "Take cover!" Officer Healey shouted, as he retreated to the safety of Boone's house. Healey had spotted a gun barrel pointed in the direction of those exposed. Two RCMP officers fired four shots—*bam, bam,* followed by *bam, bam*—in the general location of where Jim was spotted, near the living-quarters window at the back of the building, right above the extension. Their aim was to drive him back into the house rather than score a direct hit.

Their efforts met with success, presenting the gas team with a perfect opportunity.

Fitzpatrick and Argent, from their position behind the mail truck, had decided that a third shot should be attempted, this time from the western side. They, along with Taylor, who had just joined them, left their cover and ran around the front of the building, all while Jim was upstairs firing randomly. Rounding the corner, Taylor and Argent spotted civilians who were within rifle range. They quickly moved them out of harm's way.

Taylor spotted Twomey attempting to get to LeDrew and Locke. To do so would require having to pass directly into the line of fire. The choice was clear. As gunshots rang out overhead, Corporal Taylor touched Twomey on the shoulder and said, "Let's go." They raced across the parking lot, the good doctor shielded all the way by Taylor. They made it safely, and Twomey immediately went to work.

It was the perfect opportunity for Fitzpatrick, the triggerman, who had been attempting to find a suitable place and opportunity to launch the third canister. He had found cover by the porch near the western end of the building. Upon hearing the friendly fire from fellow officers, he stepped out, and from an extremely awkward angle he aimed and pulled the trigger. The canister hit the far top corner of the window and bounced harmlessly into the grass. Unsuccessful, he retreated to safety behind the porch.

Bullets fly as the Harbourview Cafe burns.
Courtesy of Juanita Thompson Chaytor.

Glancing to his right toward the trees, Ben Elliott spotted Dr. Craig making his way to assist Twomey, to do the best they could under difficult circumstances. Locke insisted on staying to fight the fire, but LeDrew's condition was critical. Dr. Craig was given the task of transporting LeDrew to the hospital by way of Ken Dean's truck as the battle continued. Twomey remained behind.

Fred Gill, a keen observer and a long-time friend of Jim Ling, watched the drama unfold. Confused by the railway ties now being placed against the two front doors, barring exit from the building, he thought, *If the idea is to have Jim surrender and come out, how can he possibly do that when escape is now impossible?* It didn't make sense to him. It was pointed out later that if Jim's intentions were to leave by the ground floor, he might have decided to simply burst through one of those doors, firing as he went. But the railway ties blocked that option. Still, today the explanation that Jim could exit those doors does not sit well with Fred Gill.

By now it was close to school time, and young Eric Edison, as he always did on school days, was strolling across the air base tarmac with some Northern Arm friends, on their way to school and totally unaware of critical events playing out farther up Water Street.

Roy Young, the author, and a mob of LeDrews were walking out Staff Road and on to Circular Road, on the way to their respective denominational schools. They saw smoke billowing from the Harbourview Cafe on their right and heard the popping of gunfire. It was frightening. Oddly enough, Roy Young began to whistle "Hang Down Your Head, Tom Dooley." It is a fact that remains in his memory today. Years later he would learn why. Similarly, hundreds of young children were dutifully marching off to classes from all parts of town, completely unaware that they may have been stepping into danger.

Around 8:30 a.m., just as the tear gas was lobbed, Nelson Jewer was headed to work down at the middle dock, which housed the distribution centre for Montreal Shipping's offices and sheds. He was driving his new Prussian Blue Morris, which he just loved and made sure to keep looking spiffy. Upon approaching the railway crossing just before reaching the café, he noticed an RCMP officer waving him down in the middle of the road. The officer opened the car door and firmly ordered, "Turn off the car and step out now!"

The officer's face was etched with strain. Nelson was slow to react. Exasperated, the officer grabbed him and dragged him down over the embankment, all while barking instructions. This was no time for conversation. "Keep your head down. Someone is inside the café, shooting. Stay there until instructed otherwise." The officer then ran back up on the road to stop other oncoming traffic.

Terrified, Nelson obeyed, totally rattled by what was unfolding in front of him. His thoughts were suddenly interrupted by the unmistakable sound of gunfire coming from inside the café. He pulled his head down farther and listened intently, all the while shaking like a leaf. Too close for comfort.

Dr. Craig, upon arriving at the hospital, ordered an amphibious aircraft out from Gander, to be used as an air ambulance to transport Fire Chief LeDrew to St. John's. The Eastern Provincial Airways plane was now heading toward the ramp on the base. Within hours of the shooting, seasoned pilots Furey, Taylor, and Rivard were on the way to St. John's with LeDrew, his wife, Myrtle, Port Superintendent Tom Antle, and Dr. Craig as attendants. Graham LeDrew would remain in St. John's for approximately six months. His arm was so mangled that only a remarkable surgeon could save his arm from amputation, and he was blessed that such a surgeon was available. They struck a deal. If he could stand the pain, the surgeon promised he would restore his arm to full use. "Let's get on with it," said LeDrew. The surgeon was indeed a man of his word.

24

Inside the Harbourview Cafe, a terrified yet defiant Jim Ling was screaming unintelligibly at the officers and volunteers surrounding the building.

He was, in the vernacular, stark raving mad. Personal relationships meant nothing now. Jim frantically ran from window to window, screeching at the top of his lungs. He was totally irrational, beyond the point of reason.

It was a pitiful scene to the many who knew and cared about Jim, and it would haunt them for the rest of their days. They wept as they watched this soft-hearted, caring man, for so many years a part of their community, now moving from window to window like a madman. For the children, their friend, their Chinese Santa, was leaving. It was truly a startling scene, causing many to whimper in sorrow. Nightmares would dog them for many years, some to their graves. The pillows of the children would be wet for many, many nights as their little minds tried to reason as to why Jim had gone away. Over half a century would pass before an answer would be forthcoming.

Incredibly, things had escalated. With a man gone crazy in a building that was set ablaze, tensions at the café reached a new level, with a very real possibility of more casualties.

Additional help had just arrived from Bishop's Falls and Grand Falls. The local firemen, volunteers, and the police, tiring from the tension, were ecstatic to see reinforcements.

Unexpectedly, the wind increased, whipping up occasional heavy gusts. There was now a very real possibility that the flames could ignite the Boone and Adams houses, and then move on to Dr. Smith's house, the company office building, and on down to the Twomeys' and beyond. If it reached as far as the police station, then it could easily burn the two schools and the Botwood Stores, wiping out everything in its path.

With this new development, an officer in the fire department directed the reinforcements, volunteers, and police manning the hoses. Additional hoses were run. "Come on, boys, step it up. Raise the angle! That's it! That's it! Now hold it there." The fight to combat the flames took on a new burst of enthusiasm and a renewed resolve to knock it down.

Old Botwood fire truck.
Courtesy of Eric Edison.

Des Simon and some of the other ten-year-old children who lived nearby had decided against going to school that morning. There was simply too much going on at the café. Unknown to their parents, some of the Nicholses, Boones, Budgells, and Woolridges crawled on their bellies in the tall grass in Frank Adams's yard, where they could get a clear view of what was going on. They saw the firemen, civilians, and RCMP officers side by side, manning the hoses. In awe, they watched as Officers Hank Johnson and Plebes climbed a single ladder on the western side, one man two rungs higher than the other, carrying a hose on their left shoulders and pistols in their right hands. The children looked on, mesmerized and fascinated. It never occurred to them that they could be in danger.

Junior Simon was watching as his father, Sam, narrowly escaped death when a bullet passed over his back, causing him to call out in surprise.

At last their efforts were rewarded, and the fire was brought under control within an hour. Thankfully, gunfire had ceased. During that hour, it took an unforgettable co-operative effort by the firefighters, police, and volunteers. Overcoming their fears, they buckled down to the daunting task. Slowly their persistence paid off, and the flames finally abated. A wave of jubilation washed over everyone, but it was short-lived. A horror show was waiting back in the café.

The fire, while under control, was still burning when the commanding officer, Inspector Argent, climbed a ladder to view the living room on the west side of the building. He peered through the smoke into the ruins and saw two bodies: one was that of Jim Ling, kneeling, with his head pushed against a chesterfield, while Ken was lengthwise on his back, lying not far from Jim's outside bedroom wall. He was lying straight out, with his arms in a contorted upward position. Ling the younger's body was a sight such as he had never witnessed before. His face was turned upwards and, mysteriously, he was stark naked in the genitalia area. Not only was the sight horrible in itself, it was atrociously gross, disrespectful, and pitiful. How could this have happened to the young man? It was impossible not to be moved. At the time, Argent couldn't imagine that pictures of father and son in such a condition would appear in the *Advertiser*, but they did, to the shock of general readers and RCMP officers alike.

Inspector Argent made some mental notes and climbed down under the watchful eyes of Fred Budgell. Fearless and curious and still feeling the chilling effects of the cold night, he ran up the ladder just vacated by Argent and peered into the room holding the bodies. He would regret that decision. The next day he squirrelled away in his room at home and penned his feelings in poetry. Many nightmares of that sight would haunt him over the years.

25

Half an hour after Inspector Argent made his observations on the ladder, the smoke had dissipated to the point that the bodies could be removed through the windows and brought to the morgue. To achieve that, the window sashes at the rear would have to be removed, as the inside of the café was extensively damaged. Hugo and Corporal Taylor climbed the ladder placed against the extension and began removing the tangle of barbed wire from the windows that Ken had installed there immediately prior to his disappearance. Next the sashes and glass would need to be cleared away. This led to an unfortunate freak accident.

Constable Crowe had climbed the ladder to the roof and asked for a shovel to break open the windows and sashes. Someone from the fire department passed him a brand-new square-top shovel with a razor-sharp edge. Crowe, for some unknown reason, his mind perhaps dulled by the madness he had just been through, grabbed the shovel by the blade and smashed it into a window sash. It brought up solid and in the process sliced into the palm of his hand, doing considerable damage. He screamed in agony and was helped down the ladder and given immediate attention by Dr. Twomey, who was still on the job. Crowe had to be transported to hospital to receive stitches to close the gash.

Once the windows were cleared away, Dr. Twomey, Inspector Argent, and Fireman Art Thompson entered. The doctor noticed that Jim's body was warm and was quivering as if it were jelly, while Ken's body appeared to be in a state of rigor mortis, indicating that he may have been dead for some time prior to Jim's death. "This, of course, will have to be determined by the

Western side of Harbourview Cafe, ladder climbed by Argent. RCMP photo.

chief government pathologist in St. John's," Dr. Twomey was overheard to say.

Others, including Tex Canning, followed them inside, and Tex also noticed that while Jim was warm and loose, Ken was ice cold and stiff as a board. Based on his years in the Swedish military, Tex was absolutely convinced that Ken had been dead for some considerable time, a day or perhaps longer.

Tex was aware of the rumours that had been circulating about the two men and speculated that Jim had indeed killed Ken and placed him in a breadbox to be disposed of later, piece by piece, if necessary.

Beneath Jim's body, Argent found a loaded shotgun, cocked and ready for action. It needed to be taken outside and discharged to release the trigger. In a considerable pool of water near the chesterfield where Jim lay was a .22-calibre gun with an expended cartridge. He called out to Corporal Foster, who was standing outside, "Take this shotgun, but be careful. The

DEATH AT THE HARBOURVIEW CAFE

Officer Foster discharges shotgun. Bodies being removed.
Schulstad photo used in *Western Star*.

shotgun is cocked and needs to be released. I'll pass you the .22 after."

Outside on the roof of the extension, Foster fired the shotgun as instructed and passed the guns to other officers to be used in evidence. He then helped Taylor and others move the bodies out onto the roof and into Ken Dean's truck. This all unfolded as hundreds of citizens looked on in disbelief. Never had they known such violence. Nobody spoke. They just stood there in stunned silence and reverence. Damage to observers was deep and permanent.

From there the remains were taken to the morgue, now once again empty. Terry Hoey's body was on its way to Peterborough, to be greeted by a devastated family and community. Ken Dean had had a very long day, as had many first responders.

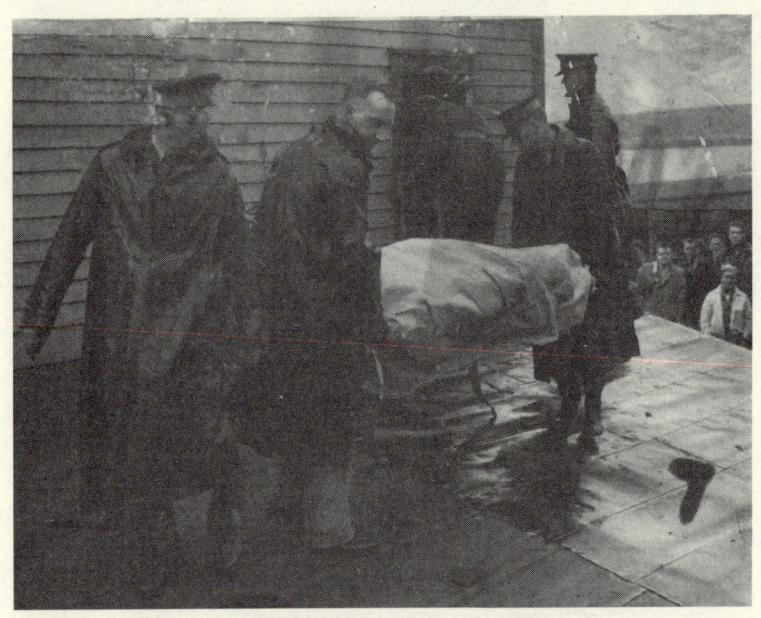

Officers removing bodies of Jim and Ken Ling. Citizens witness carnage. Schulstad of *Western Star* photo. Copies courtesy of Marie Byrne Watkins and June Peyton.

At the morgue, Jim and Ken Ling's bodies were afforded a cursory examination by Dr. Twomey. Instructions were given to the officer in charge to place the bodies in separate containers and attach identifying labels. From there these were to be shipped, along with a third container holding the breadbox, to the government pathologist, Dr. Josephson in St. John's, for autopsies to be performed. At 7:30 p.m. Taylor would accompany the undertaker from J. Goodyear & Sons to the morgue and assist him to coffin the bodies and escort them to the CNR Station in Bishop's Falls for transportation to St. John's under escort. Incredibly, the coffins would arrive mislabelled, and Immigration officials had to be called to confirm the identities.

Epilogue

During an initial search and meticulous documentation, numerous shells and personal documents as well as monetary items were located. All were taken and placed in a secure location at the police station. A police guard was placed at the smouldering café for the next twenty-four hours. This was followed by a further search and secure operation the following day.

The question on everyone's lips was, "What in hell's flames just happened to our beautiful town?" A young Mountie was dead, a long-time citizen and his son were dead, the morgue was full, the hospital was going flat out, the fire chief was in critical care in St. John's, a German sailor required plastic surgery, the Harbourview Cafe was in ruins. Adults and children alike were traumatized, and so was the rest of the province, including the provincial RCMP detachment and the national federal police force in Ottawa. Unwittingly, the entire waterfront had had a front-row seat to the carnage.

Common sense dictated that they would need to get to the bottom of this, and quickly. Surely in the wake of this disaster there would be an enquiry to help everyone find a way to cope and provide answers to so many troubling questions. Meanwhile, the town was paralyzed. Surely Mr. Smallwood's government would not let them down. No doubt the enquiry would be released in January.

Sadly, the government was given more credit than it deserved. It would take nearly sixty years for the enquiry to surface.

However, work must go on, and the A.N.D. log entry would be the first to record this regrettable historical event:

Friday, November 7th
Wind strong S.W. Sky cloudy, temperature 58 F, Barometer 29.9 falling.

A shooting incident occurred this morning at the Harbourview Cafe, when Police Constable (R.C.M.P.) Terry Hoey was shot and killed. Graham LeDrew had his arm broken at the elbow (right) and Gordon Locke had some shot in his leg. The police came from Grand Falls and Corner Brook and used gas bombs on the building after which the building caught fire. Grand Falls and Windsor fire brigade came and helped the Botwood brigade extinguish the fire. After the fire was out 2 dead Chinamen were recovered from the building.

Paper shed storing paper one truck on each shift. Ore shed not storing. Dalley and Chayter repairing shed crane. C. J. Elliott and crew repairing ore wharf rails. Jim Hayter and crew unloading tractor from schooner at the central wharf.

The café continued to smoulder. A round-the-clock police guard was put on the building, and an immediate search was carried out until nightfall. The interior of the living quarters was completely gutted by fire and considerable damage was done to the roof, particularly on the north end of the building. The whole building was searched, and quantities of money, mostly silver, along with cash in wallets, was found cached away in paper bags and cardboard boxes in various places. During the following day, November 8, 1958, a further examination was made of the building by the officer commanding, accompanied by the writer Reg Languille, who had been posted to Botwood to replace Hoey, as well as other officers. A thorough search was made for valuables, and more packages of money were found in different places in the building.

A total of $223.07 was located in both searches, found in numerous paper bags hidden in various places throughout the restaurant. As well, a black wallet belonging to Wah Tom Kent containing $20 in 1$ bills was located and stored at the detachment.

Later during the autopsy of Wah Tom Kent, another $88 was found in his clothing.

After all of the valuables and merchandise had been documented and catalogued, the building was boarded up and the security detail removed.

Late that night, a vehicle pulled up in the darkness, and for three nights following, items still there would be stolen, in particular clothing which had somehow escaped damage in the fire and water, along with beer. It became commonplace for a knock to come on people's doors and the question posed, "Are you interested in a good deal on a suit? What size do you wear?" This went on for some time, until an administrator was eventually appointed.

Café shuttered and locked. RCMP photo by Gillingham.

What remained of any value was sold at deep discounts. Then heavy equipment was brought in, and any remaining items were brought to the dump. The Harbourview Cafe was beaten down and hauled away. As bizarre as it may seem, in a matter of weeks young kids who were up at the dump site spotted a carton, and in the carton were a large number of pictures of the gruesome event, some of which are now in the author's possession, and one of which is shown. There are pictures accompanying the story that ran in the Grand Falls *Advertiser* that half a century later would never be allowed to go to press. They are gross, disrespectful, and cross the line of acceptable journalism. Being fair, at the time there were no guidelines in place as to how to deal with such a calamity, so they did what they thought was desired by the readers.

The aftermath found Gunther, the German boy, disfigured for life, and blind, that poor forgotten soul in this whole sordid affair, still in hospital on the mainland, receiving long-term specialized care. Where his life went from there is unknown, but he is spoken of often.

Graham LeDrew, one of our local heroes, was in hospital at St. John's in the course of a six-month recovery and engaged in a succession of painful surgeries which miraculously would restore the use of his arm, and he would eventually return to work.

Back in Botwood on that very day, the fire commissioner and a top-level Newfoundland Constabulary officer, uninvited by Ottawa, conducted an investigation into the RCMP, which would result in considerable conflict between the two law enforcement agencies. Terry would receive a hero's funeral, the very first to be held at the new St. Peter's Church, the one for which he and his family had worked hard to raise funds.

The body of Terry Hoey was in transit by rail, on the very same train that had carried him across Canada less than a month before. Soon he would return to the broken-hearted citizens of Peterborough and his family and many friends and colleagues. Appropriately, he would be buried November 11, Remembrance Day.

Following the funeral service, Jean Hoey, his mother,

who had given her son a word of caution in Regina upon graduation, would spot young Paddy Ryan, Terry's friend and fellow Mountie. She would pass him the unfinished letter that accompanied his personal effects when his coffin arrived, the last letter he wrote to anyone, just hours before his death.

Standing graveside among many was Stan McBride, mayor of Peterborough, who was shattered upon learning that his rising young star had come to such a sudden and violent end. Unbeknownst to Stan, Hoey's troopmate Ralph DeGroot was there, too. Remarkably, they would meet for the first time in twenty-five years on the same day, standing in the same spot.

The bodies of Tom Ling (Jim the Chinaman) and his son Wah Tom Kent (Ken, or Kim to some) were in St. John's, where autopsies would be performed to determine the cause of death. From there they would be taken to Mount Pleasant Cemetery, where they would be buried side by side in a beautiful plot with a lovely headstone, under the direction and perpetual care of loved ones who would quietly emerge and bestow on them both the filial respect for which Jim had longed so desperately. They are resting in the Chinese section a few yards from the Chinese memorial, and the memorial to Joseph R. Smallwood, whose government would leave the victims of the tragedy dangling in the wind for nearly sixty years, waiting for the results of the magisterial enquiry.

This magisterial enquiry would be called and held in Grand Falls in December 1958, under the auspices of Magistrate Cramm, the person to whom Jim reached out in vain in his time of trouble. The findings are included in this offering.

Further, Jean Hoey and her children would find comfort in their church and God and grant forgiveness for the loss of their loved one.

Over the years, troopmate Paddy Ryan would reflect on Terry Hoey at special times, like his own marriage and the upcoming birth of his first child. When the Ryans learned they were expecting, Paddy asked his wife, "If the baby is a boy, would it be okay with you if we named him Terry?"

"Yes, that would be fine," said Sylvia, but the child turned

FRED HUMBER

Dear P.G.,

How are your old stones? I arrived in Corner Brook Sub/Div. on Tuesday the 14th. and was very tired from the trip down. Although it was a real good deal, having such a long trip. When we got to Corner Brook they told us that we would be splitting up again. Attie stayed in Corner Brook on rural detachment, Getson & Brinton stayed temporarily in Corner Brook town detachment, Gaudet went to Stevenville-Crossing, Klienbub went to Stevenville, Brayley went to Grand Falls, and they put me in Botwood. As far as Reitzel & Frazer go, I am not sure just where they are. However, I did hear that Reitzel is in St. Georges, Nfld and also that Frazer is in Deer Lake. As I say though I am not sure if this is true or not. Brayley & I are only 25 miles apart. The rest of the guys are 167 miles away from us,

This place is appr. 5 or 6 thousand people, and is a three man detachment. So I will have a good opportunity to learn the work quickly. There is nothing to do down here, there is only one show in town. However, I have a very good bording house, and I like my posting very mu . The other guys here are a good bunch of heads, and they try to help me as much as they can. The N.C.O. is a married man of about 40. And the other fellow is about 23 years old. He loves hos beer, his parties , and his women. He is a lot of fun and we get out often together. There is a lot of different types of work here, as we do some town Police work, as well as our regular routine. The people here are poverty stricken, and so there is a lot of B,E,&Theft down here. I havent been in a good brawl as yet

Unfinished letter by Terry Hoey found in typewriter addressed to P. G. Courtesy of Paddy Ryan.

out to be a baby girl. But they kept with their plan and called her Terry.

Ralph DeGroot, upon retirement from the force, found himself back in Peterborough and became a volunteer to look after the graves of fallen RCMP and, incredibly, was reunited with his friend while attending to his grave and those of others. One damp November 7 morning twenty-five years after Terry's death, as he stood by the grave in reflection, he noticed a man with whom he was unfamiliar wearing a raglan against the weather. The man stepped up to him and introduced himself as Stan McBride and asked, "What brings you here today?"

Terry Ryan, daughter of Paddy and Sylvia Ryan, named in honour of Terry Hoey. Photo and permission by Paddy Ryan

Ralph explained in detail his connection to Terry and the role he was now playing.

"And why are you here?" DeGroot asked in return.

"I'm here because I am laden with guilt," was the reply. With tear-filled eyes, Stan relayed the story of how some twenty-five years before he had been largely responsible for Terry's finding himself in the Regina Depot, training to be a Mountie. He could not after all those years find resolution with the unwitting part he had played in the death of this young man. That moment was the beginning of a new friendship between the two, lasting until Stan McBride's passing. Even in death, Terry Hoey was bringing people together.

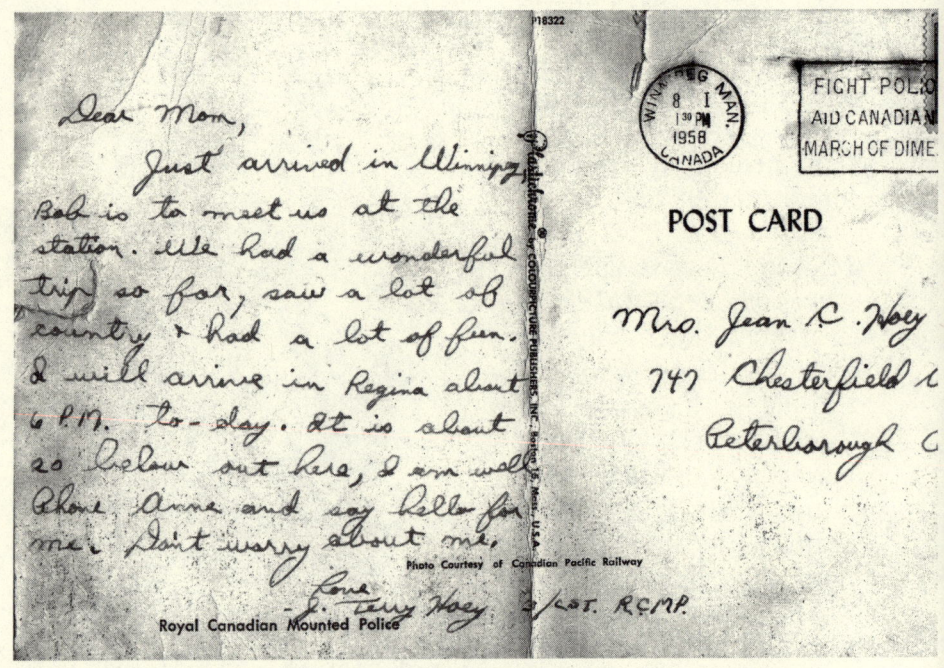

Letter Terry Hoey sent to his mom on the way to Regina Depot. Courtesy of Patricia Fryer.

It would be established that Ken was in fact married, as he claimed all along. He had gotten married in Hong Kong just before his departure to meet and reside with his adopted father, Jim Ling. They had a son named Don Tom, born in January 1955. Some years after the incident in Botwood, Ah Yee and her son travelled to Newfoundland. Due to a number of complications and regulations, they ended up residing for a while in an apartment over a business called Tom's Takeout on Gower Street in John's. Finally, in the mid-1960s, at the insistence of Tom Chow's mother, Hong Seto, they moved to Grand Falls, where they both resided at the Taiwan Restaurant with Tom and Yvonne Chow and May Soo, their daughter, and of course Hong Seto. Incredibly, she is a cousin to Ah Yee's mother back in Hong Kong. Don Tom and May Soo, both very young, became friends, and both went to school at Notre Dame Academy while Ah Yee worked at the restaurant.

Those who got to know Ah Yee describe her as a beautiful figure of a woman, and they were smitten by her personality.

Eastern side of café. Burned section tear gas fired through. RCMP photo, Gillingham.

Appendix A

In all the official RCMP reports and letters, it was categorically stated that they were never told there were guns in the Harbourview Cafe. However, it was common knowledge that Jim Ling had a gun alongside his downstairs safe, and for target practice, he spent Sunday mornings shooting gulls across the street from the café. In two reports that surfaced, Hearsey Canning clearly stated that she warned the police that there were guns in the café. On pages 207 and 208 given at the magisterial enquiry, given November 10 to Staff Sergeant Fitzpatrick, she said, "I told the Mounties [Bowen and Hoey] that Mr Ling had a gun in his quarters." When Hearsey gave a report to Fire Commissioner H. J. March, November 12, 1958, she stated that, after she climbed up the ladder to the café, ". . . I wanted to tell him [Jim] the RCMP were here. I got as far as the first two letters [syllables] and I heard like a gun cock. I did not say anything further but got down." Concern for her own safety came first, but when the police climbed the ladder, she made it clear that there was a gun in there. The RCMP conveniently ignored this person "of no outstanding virtue," a term used by Attorney General Leslie R. Curtis.

On November 17, 1958, District Inspector Harold March of the Newfoundland Constabulary, Criminal Investigation Department, penned a report to the chief of police, Mr. E. A. Pittman, pertaining to the actions of the RCMP in the November 7 historical event, that would have repercussions reaching as far as Regina. This investigation, which was ordered by the Attorney General [Leslie Curtis] unannounced to the RCMP commissioner, would cause sparks to fly with the highest-ranking officer in the Royal Canadian Mounted Police. The commissioner was livid and would make no bones about it in his return correspondence to the Attorney General. This report was separate from the magisterial enquiry and appears to be without the knowledge of Magistrate Cramm. It would lead to a series of correspondence between Ottawa and Newfoundland and is presented in its entirety so that the intensity of the event can be fully appreciated and the viewpoints of each understood against the backdrop of the times.

This is what Inspector March says in his report:

> Sir:-
> I respectfully report for your information that as instructed I visited Botwood on November 11th, 1958 (Remembrance Day and burial day of Constable Hoey) to make an investigation into the circumstances surrounding the death of Constable J. Terrance Hoey.
>
> Mr. Frank J. Ryan, Fire Commissioner who made an investigation into the cause of the fire which followed the death of Constable Hoey at the Chinese Restaurant, accompanied me to Botwood where we were met by Inspector Argent of the Corner Brook Division of the R.C.M.P. He offered me any assistance into my investigation of the death of the Constable. At the same time he informed me that his investigation was just about complete and he had covered the whole case from the beginning and would be forwarding his report to his Commanding office soon.
>
> Having knowledge of the layout of the premises in question I began my investigation by obtaining statements from the two Constables who were investigating the complaint and were present at the time of Constable Hoey's death.
>
> It appears from the information received that Tom Ling known as "Jim" operated a restaurant called the Harbourview Cafe located on Water Street in Botwood, a short distance South West of the A.N.D. Company office and assisting him were his son Tom Shang Wah usually called Ken and a waitress Miss Hearsey Canning of Botwood.

Tom Ling lived in Botwood for about twenty years but his son came to Newfoundland about four years ago. Both father and son were continually quarrelling with one another and both were reputed to be quick tempered. Neither one could speak or understand English very well and while Jim was known to leave the building only once in over a year, Ken did go out quite often. According to Miss Canning, the men hated each other, but both treated her quite well. They also treated outsiders well. This is borne out by Doctor Twomey and others of Botwood. Jim quarrelled with his son and accused him of being both lazy and crazy. It appears that he was not making money and this worried him.

This café was a resort for foreign seamen and teenagers and Jim quite often had to call Police for minor disturbances. About a month ago Ken had thrown a pan of hot fat over a German seaman and disfigured him considerably, as a result of which friends of the seaman nearly wrecked the place.

Jim had no license to sell food this year and Mr. Warrick Swyers, Health inspector for the District and a resident of Botwood, who knew Jim for years, had visited him on several occasions. On Oct. 23, he found that the place had not been cleaned to satisfactory standards, and ordered Jim to discontinue the sale of food. Jim consulted his lawyer, Mr. J.C. Higgins, and Magistrate Cramm. Decisions were slow in coming, and being naturally impatient, Jim became more worried over his business.

According to Miss Hearsey Canning, Jim blamed Ken for writing his intended wife and causing her to refuse him.

Mr. William Fong, who operated a bookstore, and had known Jim since 1940, states he was quick tempered, did not get along with his son and told him that his son would go to bed for two or three days at a time, and that he was crazy. Jim asked him to interview the doctor on his behalf to have the son certified, but Fong would not go along with the idea. Jim was worried over his business.

Dr. Twomey who knew Jim quite well stated that he thought him quite sensible and normal. But the son did not show proper filial respect according to his father and having different views they disagreed. Jim wanted him to see the son with a view of certifying him.

William Thompson who was a friend of Jim's, stated that the latter used to complain to him that the son was lazy and crazy, but he thought the boy was all right. Jim complained to him of having no business and Mr. Thompson says that it is his honest opinion that he felt Jim did not want the boy there. He did not have enough business to keep him.

Whether Jim was on the verge of a nervous breakdown as suggested by Miss Canning or just plain crazy, he appeared quite different to her on the afternoon of November 3rd past when she asked him for an hour or so off to get her hair done. About two hours later according to Mr. Frank Adams, sixty year old resident of Botwood and a neighbour and friend of Jim, the latter barred up his store at six o'clock Nov. 3rd and stated that he was sick and going to lay down. Ken the son was in the kitchen at the time. When Mr. Adams and Edgar Buckley, the only two in the store, left, that was the last time Jim opened.

For the next couple of days after that Mr. Adams when coming down his lane would call from outside the building. "Are you sick Jim? Can I get you a doctor?"

Jim would reply, "No! No! No!"

Mr. Adams further stated that both Chinamen were quick tempered and Ken was quick as a flash. They did not agree but he never saw them fight. Jim was easily upset but as good as gold. Ken was the cook.

Miss Canning goes on to say that ever since she has been working for Jim he would phone her home early in the morning and late at night, but the last time he phoned her was on Sunday night. She visited the café at

9:30 a.m. Tuesday November 4th and finding the place locked, banged on the door and got no answer. All the windows were barred from the inside and what did not have blinds were covered with ten-test. Edgar Buckley told her that Jim told him and Frank Adams the previous night that he was sick and had closed at 6 p.m.

She waited until 10:15 a.m. then went home. She phoned the place got no answer and repeated it again. She then called Mr. Frank Adams who lived next door to see if he heard anything. If one of the Chinamen had been sick she would have liked to have known it. It began to rest on her mind. She heard that Ken was going to Grand Falls on the bus Monday evening. Later enquiries from Mr. Adams revealed the fact that Jim had a fire in, so Miss Canning wondered why, if he could go down and light the fire, he couldn't answer his phone, let anyone in or talk to anyone. This had never happened before to her knowledge. She believed Jim liked her and was jealous of anyone taking her out.

On Wednesday she phoned the Police Headquarters on two separate occasions but the Police were out both times. She shortly afterwards received a call from Mr. Frank Adams and was told that Harry Chow of Windsor had been down and tried unsuccessfully to get Jim to open his café. She phoned the café again and got no answer.

On Thursday afternoon she talked with Mr. Adams again and she visited the Spot Cash operated by Mr. Harvey Fong. He advised her not to say too much to Jim as he might be crazy, but to ask him where Ken was. On the way back she spent about fifteen minutes knocking on the three doors, but getting no answer went to the rear where Mr. Adams placed a ladder against the building and she got up on the porch roof, went to the window to call to Jim. She called for quite a while before he answered her and when she asked to be let in he said "No." When she asked if Ken was in, he said, "No." and when she asked where Ken had gone he said he

DEATH AT THE HARBOURVIEW CAFE

did not know. He refused to have any further conversation. Feeling that something was wrong, she was really worried and she and Mr. Adams checked with Harvey Fong to see if Ken could be located. After some considerable checking which took till after 10:p.m. Ken could not be located between Corner Brook and Botwood. It was believed that Ken was still in the house and that something had happened to him.

Friends to the end. Jim Ling (left) and Harry Chow, revered elder of the central Newfoundland Chinese community. Courtesy of May Soo.

It was decided by Jim's friends that something was wrong with him and they would have to make a report to the Police to see what it was; if he was sick? And where the boy was: So Miss Canning notified the Police.

Harry Fong (Harvey) who was a partner of Jim's some years ago states Jim was crazy but he thought the boy was all right. He never knew him to have any firearms and neither of them drank liquor. Harry Fong (Harvey) visited Jim only twice since two years.

At this time it was thought by some of his friends that Ken was dead.

Miss Canning and her niece visited the R.C.M.P. and complained to Constables Terrance Hoey and A.A. Bowen at about 10:30 p.m. November 6th as a result of which they visited the Harbourview Cafe with the girls and tried to talk with the proprietor.

The Harbourview Cafe is of wooden frame construction. Approximately 29' by 29'. It contained a café and restaurant downstairs with a kitchen to the rear and on the second flat a large space over the café with the living quarters to the rear. These consisted of a living room 16' by 9' on the South West side of the building with one window facing South and one facing West. Off this room were two bedrooms, one at the rear of the building in line with the living room but on the side of the building and about 11 ½' by 8'. It had one window to the rear one window facing Botwood, and a second bedroom 15 ½' X 6' between the first bedroom and the storage space. This room had no window to the outside, but one cut in the partition between the bedrooms to allow light from there. There is a porch built on the rear out from the kitchen. This is of one storey and is overlooked by the rear windows of both the living room and the bedroom.

Constable Arthur Bowen of the R.C.M.P. stationed at Botwood states that Constable Terrance Hoey and himself were patrolling the town on the night of November 6th, 1958 and when passing the Detachment building about 10:30 p.m. he saw two girls at the doorway to the private quarters and recognizing one of them as Hearsey Canning, waitress at the Harbourview Cafe, he stopped the car and opened the window to hear what she wanted. She complained that Jim, the Chinaman was in the café with all the doors locked and he would not let her in. She was worried and stated that she thought Jim had killed Ken as there was no word from the latter for three days and he could not be found and Jim would give them no satisfaction.

On arrival at the café Miss Canning showed them where a ladder stood against the building and he got up to a window and tapped, calling out "Jim, this is Red the Mountie, come down and let me in." Jim appeared always glad to see him and was always very friendly. Jim did not reply for a long time, for two or three minutes, and then he said, "Go away." After a while the Constable shifted the ladder around to the side of the building to a window over the café and getting up to the window and tapping, he called Jim again and was told to go away, come back tomorrow. It was Jim's voice he heard. There was no other voice nor any noise. Constable Bowen asked what was wrong and where was Ken. Jim replied, "Ken gone away." The Constable remained there about a half hour believing he could get Jim to come out to talk to him. He told Jim that he would come in through the window if he would not come out and talk to him. It was shortly after this that Jim sneaked downstairs and crawled up again about two minutes later.

This window from where the Constable was calling looked into the storage space over the café, a large area the size of the café below. The stairway leading up from downstairs to the other side of the building was partly enclosed with a railing covered into a height of two and a half feet with the partition to the right. There was a small landing at the top of the stairs about 5' X 6' which was hidden by the partition. This is why Constable Bowen could not see if the Chinaman had anything in his hands when he crawled up the stairs. After Jim crawled upstairs (it is now believed he went to get his shot gun which he kept near the safe downstairs) he stood concealed beyond the partition and had turned off the light over the stairway and when Constable Bowen would turn off his flashlight for a second and suddenly turn it on, he would see Jim peeping around the corner at him. This happened several times and the Constable again called saying, "Jim, this is Red, none of this foolishness, come on out I want to talk with you." Jim would not come out. "Jim has gone foolish and he must have killed Ken." These circumstances worried the Constable somewhat, but he decided rather than go through the window, he would place the matter before Constable Healey who was in charge of the station. He left the premises and went to meet Healey who was on his way from Grand Falls. He told him of the circumstances and they went to the café.

Constable Healey climbed the ladder, raised the window, called to Jim several times loudly ordering him to "come here." Jim replied once, but Bowen did not understand what he said, but he saw Healey go in the building through the window. He followed and Constable Hoey followed him. Constable Healey proceeded across the room to the other side and to the small vestibule in front of the door leading to the living quarters. He rapped on the door, hollered "Jim," got no reply and tried the door, turned the knob and pushed the door open about three inches, found something like the back of a chair or chesterfield against it. He pulled it closed again. Then he called again "Jim, it's the Police," then he heard a voice inside say, "Police?" in a questioning voice and he replied "Yes, it's the Police, open the door." Constable Bowen had gone downstairs to look around to see if there was some sign of Ken who was believed to be in the building and from whom not the slightest sound had been heard. He looked in the kitchen and in the café and returned upstairs. Constable Healey was standing opposite the door frame and Constable Hoey was standing to his left directly in front of the door facing it. He said, "Let's break down the door," and had stepped back when Healey said "No," thinking he could talk the Chinaman into coming out. It was then that the shotgun was fired from the room. The charge penetrated the door about five feet from the floor and Constable Hoey staggered backwards and said, "Red, I'm shot." Constable Bowen who was only a couple of feet from Hoey coming up the stairs reached out and caught him and lowered him to the floor. Healey went to the window through which he entered and shouted for someone to get a doctor. Dr. Twomey was called. He came immediately. It was now about 12:10 a.m. Nov. 7th, 1958. Constable Bowen ran downstairs opened the door and shouted to some people outside. He returned, ran upstairs picked up Constable Hoey and brought him downstairs. Some persons entered the café and met him at the foot of the stairs and assisted in taking the body to the front of the café where it was placed on a table. Dr. Twomey who lived about a hundred yards distant arrived and pronounced life extinct. Constable Healey who had gone to the Detachment and notified Grand Falls Police returned armed. Constable Bowen then went and got his pistol and returned and they watched the living quarters to see that Jim did not escape. The general impression all around at this time was that the boy Ken was dead.

There was no doubt about the urgency of the complaint. The Police officers did their duty and went to investigate the only way they could. They contacted the proprietor, identified themselves and showed the utmost patience in dealing with him.

It can be seen that it was clearly the Chinaman's intention to talk to no one and certainly not to allow the Police or anyone else in the building. It appears he was either insane or had committed a crime. People who knew him reasoned that both answers were correct.

On the arrival of the Police from Grand Falls, the place was floodlighted and a watch was set on the building till the arrival of the police from Corner Brook who brought tear gas. The Police were augmented by crowds of people from the place, some of whom were willing to lend a hand if it were needed.

At about 8:30 a.m. the Police from Corner Brook arrived and tear gas was fired into the building. Jim, the Chinaman, having no intention of leaving the building or being taken alive, barricaded the place and decided to keep off all would-be entrants with a shot gun firing several shots and wounding a couple of persons. Jim the Chinaman had every opportunity of avoiding this incident in the first place, and even after he knew he had shot the Policeman, he could have surrendered, but he chose otherwise and died in the fire which followed.

The bodies of the two Chinese taken from the building after the fire were taken to St. John's for autopsy. The body of Constable Terrance Hoey R.C.M. Police officer of less than one year in service was examined by Dr. Twomey who issued the necessary certificate of death which had been caused by a gun shot in the left breast where a load of shot had penetrated the left ventricle of the heart and the upper chamber as well. Measurements, plans, photographs and all exhibits have been taken by the R.C.M.P. who made a complete investigation. A report of Mr. F.J. Ryan, Fire Commissioner will deal with his experiments conducted in relation to the tear gas containers used and the probable cause of the fire.

Statements enclosed forthwith.

(Sgd.) Harold March, District Inspector
E.A. Pittman, Esq., J.P.
Chief of Police.

Appendix B

The following photographs are from the RCMP investigative report.

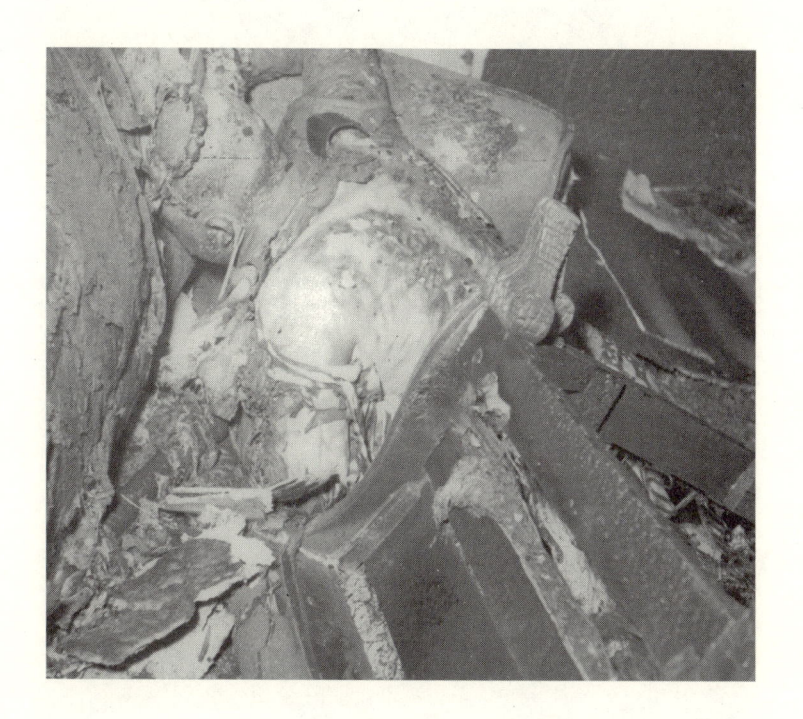

FRED HUMBER

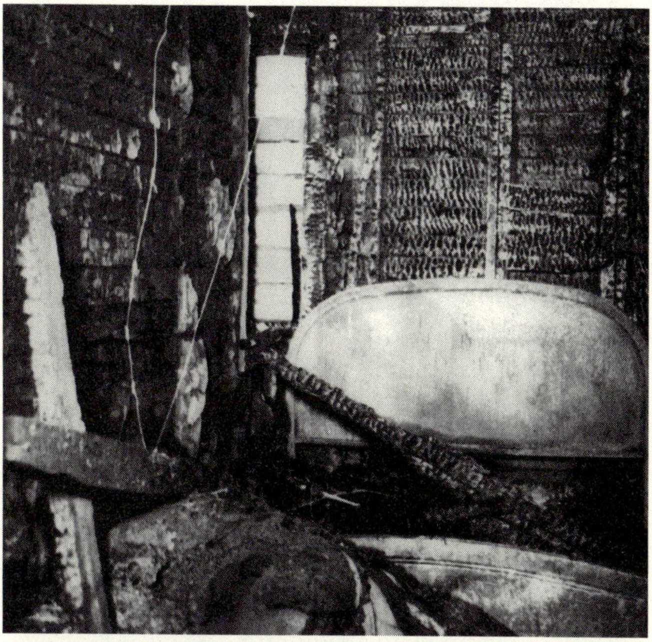

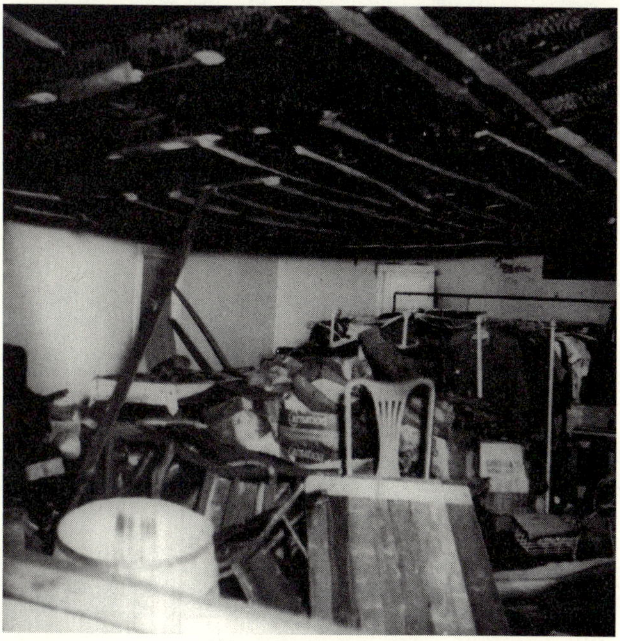

The Evening Telegram

VOLUME 80 — 140 PAGES — 15 CENTS — ST. JOHN'S, NEWFOUNDLAND FRIDAY, NOVEMBER 7, 1958 — 140 PAGES — 15 CENTS — NUMBER

TWO FIGHT TO DEATH

RCMP Constable Dies From Random Bullet

Chinese Restaurant Owner Fires Fatal Shot In Botwood Incident; Dies Later In Burning Building

Rookie Policeman Dead, 2 More Hurt

Botwood Chinese Fight Police Then Die In Fire

GUN BATTLE RAGES FOR 10 HOURS

3 Dead, 1 Wounded In Botwood Gunfight

Fatal end to young RCMP career

Barricaded Chinese Believed Killed By Tear Gas Bomb Blast

Botwood Killings Inquiry Adjourned; Doctors To Testify In Capital

GRAND FALLS (Staff) — A three-day magisterial inquiry into the Nov. 7 shooting death of Const. Terrance Hoey of Peterborough, Ont., and the deaths of two Chinese-Canadians adjourned here Thursday after four more witnesses testified.

A court official said hearings will resume "shortly" in St. John's, Nfld., where two government pathologists will release the results of an autopsy performed on the bodies of

Courtesy General Story Publ.
RCMP Const. Terry Hoey, a 2[?] Peterborough man, was kil[led in] an investigation in Newfou[ndland]. Peterborough for a mass[ive funeral] attended by RCMP officers [from across] Canada.

Shooting Enquiry Opens, Witnesses Give Testimony

RCMP Investigate Botwood Shooting

MAGISTERIAL ENQUIRY INTO FATAL BOTWOOD SHOOTING GOES INTO SECOND DAY

Botwood Slaying Inquiry Continues; Seven Witnesses Heard Wednesday

NO CONCLUSIONS REACHED YET

Probe Death Mountie, Two Chinese

Three Dead In Botwood Shooting

Police Continue Inquiry Into Triple-Death Botwood Battle

Hold Autopsy On Bodies Of Chinese

"When Did Son Die?", Autopsy May Answer

BATTLE AT BOTWOOD

Appendix C

Patricia Hoey Fryer has asked that this book include the fact that her mother and the entire family, in accordance with their Christian beliefs, have many years ago forgiven the Lings, and if there are people out there burdened by any what-ifs, or if anyone has some "secret they are going to take to the grave," then they should let it all go and enjoy what is left of their lives. Patricia and her husband, Jim, have visited Botwood and seen the memorial to her dear brother and chooses to remember the collective response of the community and the many letters written to her mother by Botwood's citizens.

Constable Terry Hoey continues to be remembered by the people of Botwood, his friends in the force, and his family, in ceremonies in Botwood and Peterborough. The RCMP syllabus would be revised to ensure that, in future, responding officers are taught not to stand in front of doors. This change in the training of recruits in Regina has without doubt saved lives over the years. The fiftieth anniversary of the Amey-Hoey Memorial Hockey Tournament was held in 2017 at Gander, Newfoundland and Labrador. Three nieces of Terry's attended, and the author had the pleasure to give them a tour of Botwood, where the tragic events took place in 1958. The town and Mayor Scott Sceviour did a magnificent job of reaching out to these ladies, and Eric Edison gave them a tour of the Heritage Museum, much to their delight. That night in Gander, Mayor Sceviour made presentations to them from the town.

Memorial in Peterborough to Terry Hoey.
Courtesy of Paddy Ryan.

Plaque to two heroes. Author photo.

Memorial Service

Constable Terrance Hoey
November 7th 2008
Peterborough, Ontario

Memorial Plaque to Terry Hoey.
Courtesy of Paddy Ryan.

Mayor Scott Sceviour second from left, author second from right, and three Hoey nieces. Courtesy of Sherri Fryer.

Hoey nieces attend fiftieth Amey Hoey Memorial Hockey Tournament in Gander, 2017. Mayor Scott Sceviour (left) presents each with a *History of Botwood*. RCMP Officer (ret'd) Law Power on far right.

FRED HUMBER

ADVERTISER, GRAND FALLS-WINDSOR, NL, THURSDAY, SEPTEMBER 2, 2010 SECTION A PAGE 3

COMMUNITY NEWS

Constable Terrance Hoey the first RCMP officer to be killed in the line of duty in Newfoundland in an incident in Botwood in November 1958, three weeks after arriving in the province.
Submitted photo

Artie Daye is well-known for his community work in the Grand Falls-Windsor area. Mr. Daye retired from the RCMP in 1981 and is currently residing in Grand Falls-Windsor. Krysta Colbourne photo

Artie Daye still holds Terry in his heart. The graduates were all like brothers. Courtesy of Artie Daye.

Artie Day continues to take every opportunity to engage in services in memory of his dear friend, participating in parades and interviews on radio and in print media. Like his troopmates, he has a deep sense of loss at the passing of his dear friend and colleague.

Canadian Police College, Rockcliffe, Ontario, will name one of its streets Hoey Road in his honour.

Botwood, Newfoundland and Labrador, will have a plaque erected in Hoey's honour just yards from where he died.

The year 2017 marks the fiftieth anniversary of the Amey-Hoey Memorial Hockey Tournament, conceived by RCMP officers to honour these two heroes killed on duty. It was held in Gander. Hoey was represented by three family members. They went to Botwood and toured the locations pertaining to the incident, including Meryl's Irving, on the site of the former Harbourview Cafe.

Legion and RCMP Hoey Memorial Parade, Botwood.
Courtesy of Artie Daye.

Meryl's Irving and coffee shop, now on the former café site.
Author photo.

Parade passes Harbourview Cafe.
Courtesy of Botwood Heritage Society.

Commanding Officer Assistant Commissioner Peter Clarke with the Hoey family at Memorial tournament in Gander. Courtesy of Sherri Fryer.

DEATH AT THE HARBOURVIEW CAFE

Officer Terry Hoey receives an honour guard. Peterborough falls silent in shock and sorrow as a hero is laid to rest in St. Peter's Cemetery, the first funeral in the brand new church. He will not be forgotten there nor in Botwood. Peterborough *Examiner*, November 11, 1958.

Appendix D

Jim (Tom Ling) and Ken (Wah Tom Kent) received the filial respect of the teachings of Confucius from an unexpected source, Don Tom, the son of Ken and Ah Yee. This comes in the form of perpetual care for them as they lie side by side at Mount Pleasant Cemetery in St. John's. Respect for one's ancestors continues to be at the core of Chinese consciousness. Respect is everything.

The Harbourview Cafe, Jim Ling's "Gold Mountain," was subsequently torn down. A garage and gas bar was built on the site. Over the years it underwent several changes, and today it is Meryl's Irving, a popular gas bar and coffee shop.

Mount Pleasant Cemetery
Tom Ling
Wah Kent Tom
Buried in Section C South #3
Plot 134, Graves 2 and 3
Located on lower side down from where Joey Smallwood is buried
Chinese monument near Joey Smallwood's grave

The writer was afforded the honour of being invited by May Soo to attend the Annual Flower Service held at Mount Pleasant Cemetery in St. John's. It takes place every year on the Sunday following Regatta Day. Chinese citizens pour in from across the province to honour their

William Fong attending flower service.

ancestors and become reacquainted with one another. Amazed, I watched with May and her mom, Yvonne Chow, as they gathered at the Chinese Memorial for prayers. Following this, we participated in a meal at graveside in respect for the dearly departed. They do indeed honour their ancestors. It was a remarkable experience.

Most of the Botwood Chinese citizens of the day have passed and are buried in Mount Pleasant in the Chinese section near the monument. Mrs. Victor (Boey Chee) Wong and Mrs. William (Shirley) Fong remain in Botwood, as do Jean Jine, daughter of Harvey and Winnie Fong, and Jean's son, Johnny. Many offspring of the Chinese will acquire the education so highly valued and will move away to become practising professionals and contributing members of society, thus fulfilling the wishes of their parents and in accordance with the teachings of Confucius.

Father and Son lie side by side in peace.
Author photo.

Appendix E

Gunther, the forgotten German boy, did not return to Botwood. Over the years, many people wondered where he went and how his life turned out following the brutal and unexpected attack by Ken at the café. They will never forget the song "Western Movies" by The Olympics. It can be found on YouTube. The song was simple enough and never became a hit of any consequence, yet the incessant playing of the song on the Harbourview Cafe jukebox would precipitate the following:

> A young man from Germany maimed for life.
> The first R.C.M.P. officer to die in the line of duty in Newfoundland.
> The deaths of two Chinese citizens.
> The wounding of two non-Chinese citizens.
> Botwood traumatized for decades.
> A Magisterial Enquiry held and its finding withheld and undiscovered for fifty-eight years.
> Maligned individuals.
> Amendment to the RCMP syllabus used in the Training Depot in Regina.

Dr. Hugh Twomey would go on to fulfill an outstanding career in medicine and later in politics. In the latter role he would influence the construction of a chronic care health centre built in Botwood, which was named in his honour and became a major employer in the community and provided continuing care to those he came to serve so many years ago. Further, an outstanding mural honouring Dr. Twomey and the hospital staff was erected and can now be seen on the site where the hospital once stood.

Pulse of the community. Mural reproduced is the exclusive property of and with the permission of the Botwood Mural Arts Society Inc. Mural Artist Charlie Johnston, Winnipeg. Depiction of Dr. Twomey and the staff at the Botwood Cottage Hospital.

Graham LeDrew would recover and return to work and live to retirement. He is rightfully recognized as a hero.

Those of us left standing who were children on November 7, 1958, are now advancing in years and are seniors. Times have changed, and no doubt the young people of today are having their own great times which they will carry with them into adulthood. However, they should know—they deserve to know—just what took place in their town so many years ago.

The RCMP *Quarterly* (volume 24, no. 3) states, "The complete story leading up to his [Hoey's Reg. No 20307] untimely death will, however, likely remain forever a mystery hidden deep in the mystic crevices of an oriental mind."

Perhaps not so mystical after all. Perhaps a reflection of our ignorance at the time of the many racist pressures at play along with the depth of entrenchment of filial piety in the lives of Chinese people, to which they aspired.

The magisterial enquiry finally got to see the light of day fifty-eight years later, providing many answers and posing yet more questions. Over the years many, including the writer, would ask why that was the case. Why we were denied? It is difficult to accept the suggestion offered by one individual in the archives that "perhaps you are the only one that ever asked for it." Perhaps the answer lies deeper.

Fire Chief Graham LeDrew. Courtesy of Reg LeDrew.

On December 31, 1958, less than two months after the tragedy, a strike would be called involving the Newfoundland loggers and the A.N.D. Company. The loggers had requested representation from the International Woodworkers of America to overcome third-world working conditions to which they were subjected by the company. They had had enough of sleeping on spruce boughs, eating baked beans six days a week, contending with bedbugs, having to go in the woods to use the bathroom, and having no place to shower or bathe. Some say conditions were far worse in the camps than that experienced by criminals incarcerated at Her Majesty's Penitentiary. They had much in common with the early Chinese labourers in the gold fields and on the railway, with no one to turn to.

Premier Joseph R. Smallwood was enraged by the notion that the IWA, led by a silver-tongued H. Landon Ladd, had the gall to oppose the toothless Newfoundland Loggers Union, over which he held a clenched steel fist. Referring to them as gangsters and communists, he enacted legislation decertifying the IWA, leaving the neutered NLU still in power. Moreover, all the issues which were previously considered non-negotiable by the company and which were the basis on which the IWA took a stand were suddenly approved under the NLU. One would have to be blind not to see through it.

This scandalous collusion led to the NLU and its affiliate being banished by the Canadian Labour Congress and an unrepentant Smallwood soundly rebuffed by the federal government. This was, after all, a free country and not a dictatorship.

In the wake of all of this, a savage incident occurred at Badger while members of the RCMP and Newfoundland Constabulary stood together side by side in the hope of preventing violence on the picket line.

On March 10, 1959, it would cost the life of Newfoundland Constabulary Officer Constable William Moss and cause a rift within formerly closely knit logging families and the province in general that would last for decades, and in some cases it exists today. Perhaps "the hopefully cold news" regarding the Botwood incident referred to in the Attorney General's letter to the commissioner of the RCMP was best kept under wraps, as it could be additional fuel to an already raging inferno of a government already under the microscope. Was there any value to its release? Perhaps not to the politicians of the day, but certainly it was to those directly involved.

Since November of 1958, much has been learned about the many faces of mental illness and its treatment, and about the effects of what would eventually be called post-traumatic stress on witnesses and first responders. Such knowledge would have played a huge part in events leading up to the triple tragedy and in dealing with the aftermath.

The need for specialized squads of police, trained to deal with high-tension and lethally dangerous situations, has been recognized, developed, and deployed, and training continues to be modified. Officers now carry real weapons rather than the riding crops that were used as tokens of weapons.

The writer holds the deepest respect for our police officers, those special people who risk their lives to protect our citizens. This offering is an attempt to understand what happened leading up to and including that fateful night. It must be examined in the context of the times in which it happened. Thankfully, so much has changed since then.

Appendix F

Below is Terry Hoey's letter to his mother while on the way to Regina RCMP Depot to commence training.

> January 8, 1958
> Winnipeg Man.
> 1:30 p.m.
>
> Dear Mom,
> Just arrived in Winnipeg. Bob is to meet us at the station. We had a wonderful trip so far. Saw a lot of country and had a lot of fun. I will arrive in Regina about 6 p.m. today. It is about 20 below out here. I am well. Phone Anne and say hello for me. Don't worry about me.
>
> Love,
> J. Terry Hoey
> 3rd Constable
> R.C.M.P.

Terry left an unfinished letter in the typewriter addressed to P. G. on November 6, 1958. Many versions of its contents were in circulation in the rumour mill. The letter was received by Terry's mother, Jean Hoey, with his personal effects. She recognized to whom the initials referred. She found Paddy Ryan, a troopmate of Terry's, and gave it to him. He kept it, realizing how very special it was. When he heard of the author's project, he sent along a copy of the letter and other reference materials.

Dear P.G.,

How are your old stones? I arrived in Corner Brook Sub/Div. on Tuesday the 14th. and was very tired from the trip down. Although it was a real good deal, having such a long trip. When we got to Corner Brook they told us that we would be splitting up again. Artie stayed in Corner Brook on rural detachment, Getson & Brinton stayed temporarily in Corner Brook town detachment, Gaudet went to Stevenville-Crossing, Klienbub went to Stevenville, Brayley went to Grand Falls, and they put me in Botwood. As far as Reitzel & Frazer go, I am not sure just where they are. However, I did hear that Reitzel is in St. Georges, Nfld and also that Frazer is in Deer Lake. As I say though I am not sure if this is true or not. Brayley & I are only 25 miles apart. The rest of the guys are 167 miles away from us.

This place is appr. 5 or 6 thousand people, and is a three man detachment. So I will have a good opportunity to learn the work quickly. There is nothing to do down here, there is only one show in town. However, I have a very good boarding house, and I like my posting very much.

The other guys here are a good bunch of heads, and they try to help me as much as they can. The N.C.O. is a married man of about 40. And the other fellow is about 23 years old. He loves his beer, his parties, and his women. He is a lot of fun and we get out often together. There is a lot of different types of work here, as we do some town Police work, as well as our regular routine. The people here are poverty Stricken, and so there is a lot of B, E & Theft down here. I haven't been to a brawl as yet.

There were many people, some directly involved in the events, who believed the *Germont* was the ship involved in the fat incident. Others thought it was the *Germa*. With the help of Ted

Mills's incredible memory and using the A.N.D. logbook, the author was able to discern that it was actually the *Alstertal*, a German ore carrier making her first trip when the incident occurred. Some say she did resemble the *Germont*, a Norwegian vessel which was nowhere near Botwood during the time of the events unfolding.

The SS *Alstertal*. Walter E. Frost photo, courtesy of Paul Willie.

The Spot Cash businesses flourished to a point that enabled both Harvey and Charlie to attain the unthinkable: new cars. Harvey had done some research, so he took the lead as he and Charlie went to Grand Falls to buy vehicles.

They drove up to their chosen dealership, and Harvey went inside and spoke to a salesperson about the particulars of a specific model and decided yes, this was the right one. Harvey declared he was impressed and informed the salesman he wanted to buy two.

The salesman thought Harvey was putting him on and dismissed him, replying, "Why not take six?" and immediately turned his attention to another customer.

Despite the sleight, Harvey waited for the salesman to return to deal with him, but after five minutes, he'd had enough. He grabbed his hat and drove to a different dealer. Before leaving this dealer, he had purchased two top-of-the-line, lime-green Dodge Desotos. Today, all the older folks in Botwood remember those huge Dodge Desotos.

Through the grapevine, the owner of the other dealership heard about what had happened. He put a notice placed under glass in the showroom that went along these lines:

Attention All Staff

Be advised that anyone coming on our property has not done so looking for shirts, shoes or groceries. They are here looking for what we sell. Automobiles. Our jobs and futures depend on our selling automobiles. Therefore, we all need to pay attention to these people and find out what specifically they are looking for and to help them find it. That may mean a number of things like directing them to a salesman, the service department or management. That is to say we must treat them like we want to be treated ourselves, with the greatest respect. In so doing we will be in business this year and many years to come. Our jobs, yours and mine, depend on it.

Please pay attention and remember that we are here to serve. Otherwise people will take their business elsewhere, as we have found out just recently.

Sincerely, President

In 1951, Harvey traded his lime-green vehicle for a new model when his wife and daughter Jean came over from China. The soul-crushing rules barring female Chinese from entering Canada had changed, as a consequence of the United Nations Declaration of Human Rights. This time the new car was pink, an acknowledgement of his happiness to at last have his wife, and Jean, the daughter whom he had never seen, finally home with him under the same roof. It was a struggle to get there, though. Soon his home was filled with the cries of new babies arriving into a life of opportunity. Harvey was so very happy, and it reflected in his demeanour.

Some thought that Hearsey was largely responsible for the death of Terry as well as Jim and Ken. Evidence does not line up with this allegation. Rather, it is clear that she had a deep and positive relationship with both Chinamen based on a demonstrated respect toward them, beginning with teaching them English and defusing hostilities between them whenever possible. For days she and Linda, her niece, made an extraordinary effort to communicate how close each of the Lings was to resorting to violence against one another. Hearsey knew things that no one else did, which convinced her that such was the case. She believed, as did Linda, that if someone had listened to her at the outset, when she tried to explain this, things might have turned out quite differently. People paid her no heed.

They both were dismissed by everybody until the last minute, when finally it was realized that something was amiss. At that point she was finally given clearance to contact the police. That came in the evening, in November darkness. Face-to-face contact was made with police, at which point it became a police matter. Decisions made thereafter were not hers to make.

She informed the police regarding a gun in the building, while in the cruiser and several times at the scene, screaming out her warning through cupped hands. Again she was being dismissed. One has to ask, at what point does the responsibility for a minimum-wage young girl "of no outstanding virtue," to quote the Attorney General, having no status within the community, end? More importantly, when does someone else's responsibility begin?

Was she the only one in town who knew about the café being locked and shuttered and of the tension between the two? Clearly, she was not. Further, she and Linda walked for miles, calling on those with status, hoping for some collective action leading to a peaceful resolution, and that applied to both Caucasian and Chinese citizens. Not to worry, essentially, was the response she received. This was likely just another "withdrawal," as had happened previously. Nothing new here.

She valued her friendship with the Lings and had core values learned at home which would not permit her to abandon them in what she perceived as "their hour of need," even to the point of climbing on the roof of the coal shed, knowing Jim had a gun inside. She trusted her friendship with Jim to prevail and thus ensured he knew that it was "Boey" that was speaking to him. But he was mentally ill at the time and could have pulled the trigger. Hearsey Canning put her life on the line for the Lings. She, too, was a hero.

The Chinese community in Vancouver certainly were of the opinion that decisions made after that were police decisions and let the RCMP know it in no uncertain terms.

In the aftermath, Hearsey became the recipient of considerable abuse by some people. When she went out, she would sometimes be accosted by other young women. They would say things to her like, "You shouldn't have gone down there. Oh, maid, what did you go down there for?"

A tearful, devastated Hearsey would reply, "You know, they were my friends. We were worried about them."

This usually brought a terse, "My dear, you're foolish," which broke her heart. After all she had done to have someone come forward to help, all in vain.

One night, Linda had heard enough. Seeing her aunt on the verge of tears again, she looked directly at the abuser. "She should have ignored them like everybody else did, I suppose! Just go about your own business, I suppose! After all, it's only Jim the Chinaman! Justify your doing nothing by criticizing someone who did? You and people like you make me sick."

The abuse cut Hearsey deeply, but over time it did diminish somewhat after that telling-off. Nonetheless, she knew what they were thinking. Never did she believe she had done the wrong thing. She also knew something that they did not. She had told the police there was a gun in the building.

There was no unanimity on whether or not the officers should have entered. Witness the exchanges between the commissioner of the RCMP and the Attorney General's office:

> December 2, 1958
> R.C.M.P. Superintendent Reports of Commissioner L.H. Nicholson
>
> ... In this connection, both Mr. Curtis and Mr. Puddester considered that there might be criticism leveled at members of the Force going to the Chinese Quarters when they did, and also there might be criticism of the fact that this Force was the only investigating agency into the death of one of our members.

Attorney General L. R. Curtis writes to RCMP Commissioner. In part:

> Feb 25, 1959
>
> As soon as I learned that both the chinamen were in Botwood and alive at the time of the Botwood incident, I feared that some of this resentment, resentment which I feel is quite unfair and unwarranted, might flare up, so, in order that I might have something that I could use in defence of the R.C.M.P., I instructed a high ranking officer of the Newfoundland Constabulary to check on what had happened in Botwood...
> ... I was worried lest the R.C.M.P. be accused of acting too promptly and ill-advisedly during the wee small hours of the morning and during the hours of darkness they endeavoured to enter the restaurant. It is always easy to be wise after the event, and I think that the officers concerned will agree with me now when I suggest that if they had deferred this entry until the next morning the results would not have been as disastrous as they were. I realize, of course, that feelings were running very high in Botwood, particularly after Constable

Hoey's death, but it does seem to me the need for haste was unduly stressed by the woman in the case, a character of no outstanding virtue.

It has at no time been emphasized publicly that both these Chinese were in the building and alive at the time the attack took place and time in this case is on our side. Evidence to this effect has not yet been given publicity, and when it does come out the news story, as a story will be cold. This at least is my hope. You will be glad to hear I know that the report of the Newfoundland Constabulary officer was very satisfactory. It has never been released for publication and will not be so released except when such release is in the interests of the R.C.M.P. I am not looking for trouble; I am trying to anticipate it.

See below the scathing letter from the Chinese Benevolent Association in Vancouver, BC, to the RCMP in Ottawa.

The incident was indeed news across the nation. The Chinese Benevolent Association in Vancouver heard of it and immediately lodged a complaint with the RCMP, believing that it was unwarranted and they were seeking a response. It was their role to look after the best interests of the Chinese citizens of Canada. They carried their objection in their own newspaper and contacted the RCMP in Ottawa directly, seeking answers. Their objection is stated verbatim below.

> Foreign Language Press Review Service,
> Department of Citizenship and Immigration,
> Canadian Citizenship Branch
> Newspaper: The *Chinese Voice*, Vancouver Nov 25, 26/58
>
> The Chinese Benevolent Association is concerned about the incident in Newfoundland.
>
> On November 7, two Chinese and a Mounted Police were killed in an incident in Botwood, Newfoundland. The two Chinese were father and son and were the owners of a restaurant. The restaurant was closed for sev-

eral days for some unknown reason. An employee of the restaurant called the police and three policemen came and forced their way into the restaurant at two a.m. One of the Chinese fired a shot from upstairs and killed one policeman. The police then burned the restaurant and the two Chinese burned in the fire. The Association is greatly concerned about this incident and has retained a lawyer to look after this matter. It is felt that the police should not have forced their way into the restaurant in the middle of the night and they should not have set fire on the premises.

(To RCMP and the Deputy Minister of Justice)
Received December 22/58

The issue referred to in this complaint would in fact be addressed in the magisterial enquiry. One presumes that the Association got what the people of Botwood did not, namely a copy of that enquiry. There is no record to substantiate this. Perhaps they were treated as disrespectfully as everyone else by the government.

Appendix G

On November 11, the fire marshal conducted various tests on the tears-gas canisters and projectiles regarding combustion points. There was some speculation that Jim might have set the fire himself in his wild rage and in an attempt to go to his death in a blaze of glory. The fire marshal would conclude that the tear-gas implements could have and likely did cause the fire. Prevention and combatting of a potential fire was in the minds of the police. They had contacted the fire department in advance, just in case a fire should start. However, it was not the intent to burn Jim out with flames, but rather to dislodge him with tear gas. It was intended to prevent loss of life and take him into protective custody before he could cause any more loss of life or injury.

It appeared that Ken was being prevented from leaving by some hold his father had over him. There was indication that Ken was placed or ordered into a large cardboard box upstairs, where his body was later found. There may have been threats made against him by his father to stay there and be quiet, as the existence of guns was well-known to Ken, and he knew that Jim was quite capable of using them.

On November 18, 1958, Fire Commissioner Frank J. Ryan would write to the Attorney General regarding the fire and give the following observations.

Regarding various tests he had undertaken with the tear-gas grenades and canisters, "I have concluded that the shells and grenades used in the operations at the Harbourview Cafe could cause fire and possibly did set fire to the building.

". . . but if carbon monoxide has been discovered in the

lungs of the son, it is reasonable to assume that both he and his father died in this fire.

"Finally, I will state that from my observations and investigation of this fire, I am of the opinion that tear-gas shells and grenades used in this instance were capable of starting this fire and that there is the possibility that both father and son died through the fire, unless the postmortem examinations determine otherwise."

Appendix H

According to Inspector Arthur Argent of the RCMP Corner Brook Subdivision in a report forwarded November 20, 1958, to Officer Commanding "B" Division, events leading up to the deaths of Constable Hoey and Jim and Ken Ling and the wounding of LeDrew and Locke were many and complex.

> Tom Ling had become mentally unbalanced morose and became dangerous to the public at large, and his self-imposed exile in the withdrawing of all public contact by locking up his Cafe and retreating to his living quarters created the concern shown by some of the local populace at Botwood that culminated in official complaints relative to the matter being made to this Force at Botwood. Tom Ling known to be of an excitable nature and quick tempered appeared to be antagonistic towards his son Tom Wah Kent and was known to have passed comments that he hoped he would go away as he was not good for business at Botwood. Further, he blamed his son for interfering and upsetting arrangements he had instituted for a Chinese woman to come from China whom he intended to marry. That element of ill will existed between these two Chinese can be accepted as fact.
>
> Briefly, Tom Ling and his son Tom Wah Kent were last seen together in the kitchen . . . he was in addition in major conflict with his son, whom he wished would go away since he was a detrimental effect on business. Further, the Harbourview Cafe on the evening of November 3rd, at which time Tom Ling was considered to be un-

usually quiet. And reserved in manner. Tom Wah Kent appeared quite normal and had apparently planned to go later that evening to Grand Falls to attend a picture show. From the evening of November 3rd the Cafe remained locked up and all contact with Tom Wah Kent ceased, either voluntarily on the part of the son or some form of compulsion from the older Chinaman.

Attempts to make contact with Tom Ling by telephone and personal appeals by close neighbours, an employee and a Chinese café owner from Windsor, all disposed to be friendly were fruitless in effect and resulted only in the information that Tom Wah Kent had gone away; that Tom Ling spoke savagely in an incoherent manner and the Chinese Harry Chow expressed his opinion that Tom Ling was mentally unbalanced. Further inquiries undertaken by local Chinese for Tom Wah Kent led to the belief that he had not left Botwood and grave concern was expressed for his safety.

The decision to enter the café was undertaken only after considerable discussion by the police officers concerned, their object being to ascertain the whereabouts of Tom Wah Kent and necessary to take into custody Tom Ling as a mentally ill person and their action appears to be well within the broad provisions of Section 278 of the Health and Public Welfare Act, Chapter 51 of the revised statutes of Newfoundland.

That Tom Ling was mentally unbalanced appears substantiated by his reckless shot through the doorway of his living room that struck and killed 3rd Cst. Hoey after having been fully and adequately advised that it was the police seeking to gain entrance.

In advancing the theory that Tom Ling was mentally unbalanced it is inconceivable to believe that Tom Wah Kent at the same time had likewise become mentally unbalanced also and was in full cooperation with the older Chinese. All evidence points to these two Chinese being antagonistic to one another and presuming Tom Wah Kent was mentally normal it would appear that some form of duress was imposed upon him that rendered him incapable of making his presence known.

Following the shot that killed 3rd Cst. Hoey and up until the time of the first gas shell being fired, not another shot was fired either by police or armed civilians and during this period intermittent calls to Tom Ling were made by police and local residents well known to the Chinese to surrender with guarantee of safe custody but no response to these overtures were made.

There being no alternative but to take Tom Ling into custody as expeditiously as possible before he had further opportunity to harm the police or the public at large, the decision was made to use tear gas which provided maximum chance to accomplish this objective with the minimum of further violence.

Following the firing of the second gas shell into the east bedroom window and whilst a shot gun was being fired from the north living room window, a reflection of fire was observed inside the east bedroom which spread almost instantaneously into a sheet of flame that in a matter of seconds enveloped the whole room.

This fire subsequently did major interior damage to the two bedrooms and living room occupied by the two Chinese and considerable damage to the roof before being brought under control.

The cause of this spontaneous fire is not known and I personally have no knowledge of any previous fire being occasioned by the use of tear gas. It is known that tear gas grenades generate considerable heat in the canister with the object to prevent the canister from being picked up and thrown back, however, where the two grenades were used no fire took place. The gas shells do not heat in the same manner and it appears impossible for one of these shells to ignite a room into spontaneous combustion even under ideal conditions. That the possibility exists that the Chinese Tom Ling may have started the fire in his determination to perish rather than submit to arrest cannot be overlooked.

During the whole incident it has been definitely ascertained that no shots were fired by the police in their endeavour to effect the arrest of Tom Ling until within the last minute, when Csts. Healey and Saunders each fired two shots at the west living room window when they noticed a gun barrel levelled in the direction of police personnel endeavouring to aim another gas shell into the building and whom they considered were momentarily in eminent danger. None of these four bullets inflicted any injury to the Chinese who by the Death Certificate died of asphyxia due to smoke. A shot gun loaded with ball shot and cocked was found cupped in the arms of Tom Ling on the chesterfield in such a position that same could have been used from this very point to fire out of the west living room window and it can be presumed that the combined effect of gas and fire had immobilized him from discharging the weapon.

It might be stated that the restraint and standard of discipline displayed by all police personnel and civilian cooperation was excellent.

Much credit is due to Mr. Graham LeDrew, Botwood Fire Chief, who while working in close cooperation with the police, discarded his place of safety on the first alarm of fire to run for the hose when he was struck by a ball shot in the right arm fired by the unfortunate man whom the Fire Chief was trying to save from his peril.

Instructions relative to the Magisterial Enquiry are duly awaited, all witnesses with the exception of Mr. LeDrew now hospitalized at St. John's, are available.
STILL UNDER INVESTIGATION

(A. Argent) Insp. Comdg. Corner Brook S/Divn.

Appendix I

RCMP Staff Sergeant J. G. Fitzpatrick to the Officer Commanding "B" Division:

> As soon as the fire was brought under control and before it was actually out the Officer Commanding climbed a ladder and looked in through the window of the living room on the west side of the building. Although there was considerable smoke at the time he was able to discern two bodies in the room. One, that of the older man was sprawled face downward on a chesterfield, in a sort of kneeling position with that portion of the body from the waist up resting on the chesterfield. The clothing had been burnt off the back to below the buttocks but no major fire damage had been done to the body and the features were clearly discernible. At that time what appeared to be another body was observed lying face up and extended straight along the south wall of the living room. (Photographs were taken after these observations made and the fire actually out).
>
> Within approximately half an hour after the above observations were made and the smoke cleared away sufficiently the bodies were removed from the locations and brought to the hospital. Then the body of Tom Ling was removed from its original position and a loaded 12 gauge shot gun was taken from underneath him. The gun was cocked at the time. An effort was made to release the trigger without discharging the gun, when it was found that this was impossible the gun was taken outside the

building and discharged. Following the removal of the water which at that time was about 18 inches deep on the floor of the living room a .22 single shot rifle was found on the floor close to the chesterfield and near the doorway leading to the passageway. An expended .22 cartridge was still in the breach of the rifle. The items referred to will be the subject of exhibit reports.

After the bodies of the two Chinese were removed to the morgue they were viewed by Dr. Twomey. At that time Cpl. D.G. Foster removed 8 loaded 12 gauge shot gun shells together with 20 one dollar bank notes from the pocket of the clothing of Tom Ling. Six of the 12 gauge shells were loaded with no. 4 shot and two were loaded ball ammunition.

On instructions from Officer Commanding "B" Division the bodies of the two Chinese were shipped to the Government pathologist at St. John's Nfld. for post mortem examination. Caskets for this purpose were obtained from J. Goodyear & Sons Ltd. of Grand Falls, Nfld. The bodies were escorted from Botwood to Bishop's Falls, Nfld. by Cst. F.E.S. Barton who accompanied them to St. John's via the C.N. Railway. The autopsy report of the Pathologist has not yet been received.

Appendix J

<u>JOSEPH JOSEPHSON</u>-Sworn

I am a registered Medical Practitioner and Government Pathologist. I am a Graduate of the Medical School of Queens University Kingston Ontario, of 1934 and have been practising the specialty of Pathology for the past twenty years.

On November 8th, 1958 I performed post-mortem examinations on the bodies of Tom Wah Kent and Tom Ling, both Chinese subjects. These bodies were identified to me by Mr. L.J. Payne, Immigration Officer in charge. Tom Wah Kent was a young slender Chinese male, five feet three inches in height and weighing approximately 115 pounds. The clothing over the front half of the body was extensively burnt, but it showed no blood stains or unnatural marks. The skin over the face was superficially charred and blackened by burning while much of the hair had been singed, and part of the front and side of the scalp superficially burnt. Both hands were extensively scorched and the skin over the fingers and palms of the hands loosened. Following removal of the clothing, areas of superficial burning were found on the skin over the front of the chest and legs and genitalia. The backs of the trunk and legs and the inner aspects of the thighs were not burnt. Aside from several small closely aggregated blue and red ante mortem bruises on the back of the upper third of the left upper arm, in an area measuring two inches in diameter, there was no evidence of any other traumatic injuries or marks of violence, and in particular no gunshot wounds. There were no scratches or injection marks such as might have been made by hypodermic needle. There was a large broad smear of light yellowish material closely resembling yellow paint adherent over the skin and the left shoulder and front of the chest measuring six by four inches, and several small patches of similar material were spattered on the front of the chest. Pin head sized spatters of similar yellow paint like material were irregularly distributed on the back of the right hand and fingers. No paint was found on either of the two T shirts clothing the body and none was noted on the partially burnt trousers. Upon opening the body a cherry pink discolouration of the arterial blood and all the tissues was obvious. This finding is consistent with carbon monoxide poisoning. A considerable amount of inhaled black sooty material was applied to and irregularly distributed through the mildly congested inner lining of the trachea (windpipe) and bronchial tubes (the lower passages in the lungs). In addition there was a mild edema (swelling) of the epiglotic folds (folds over the vocal cords). A few tiny superficial hemorrhages of the asphyxia type were scattered on the surface of the lungs. Both lungs were acutely congested and moist. The organs elsewhere including the brain showed some acute congestion plus the cherry pink discolouration already noted. There was no evidence of any internal injury or significant natural diseases. The skull and other bones were intact. A chemical examination of blood taken from the right side of the heart revealed a carboxyhaemoglobin content in excess of 10%, which is indicative of carbon monoxide intoxication. No alcohol was present. As our laboratory is not equipped to analyze samples of opiates, appropriate specimens of liver, kidney, blood, and urine were passed over to the R.C.M.P. for submission to their Toxicology Laboratory for this analysis. Microscopic examination of the tissues by me here revealed no further points of significance and certainly no disease processes which might be construed as a cause of death.

The autopsy upon the body of Tom Ling revealed a 56 year old male Chinese subject who was fairly obese, weighing approximately 180 pounds, and who measured five feet five inches in height. The clothing both back and front had been extensively burnt. The tip of the tongue protruded a short distance from the mouth and was tightly clenched between the teeth. The skin over the face, the back, and the front of the trunk, lower limbs and hands were superficially charred and scorched in many areas. There was no evidence of any traumatic injury nor gun shot nor needle marks or scratches noted anywhere on the body. Neither was there any paint such as was observed on the skin of the body of Tom Wah Kent. Internal examination revealed a distinct cherry pink discolouration of the arterial blood and of all the tissues. A large amount of inhaled black sooty material was adherent of the lining along the entire length of the upper and lower air passages which were also moderately inflamed and irritated. There was a slight edema of the larynx. The lungs showed a marked degree of acute congestion and were quite moist. The organs elsewhere including the brain showed acute congestion and the cherry pink discoloration already noted. There was no evidence of any injury or any significant natural disease. The skull and other bones were intact. Chemical examination of a sample of blood from the right side of the heart of Tom Ling also revealed a carboxyhaemoglobin content in excess of 10% indicating carbon monoxide intoxication. No alcohol was present. Samples similar to those in the case of Tom Wah Kent were passed over to the R.C.M.P. for submission to their toxicology laboratory for analysis for opiates. The microscopic examination of the tissues from Tom Ling also revealed no other points of significance, and certainly nothing which might be considered the cause of death.

In my opinion the high content of carboxyhaemoglobin in the sample of the heart's blood and the presence of a large amount of inhaled soot material through the slightly irritated air passages in the case of both Tom Wah Kent and Tom Ling clearly establishes that both these subjects were alive and breathing at the time of the fire and that death was definitely due to asphyxiation by smoke. Smoke from a conflagration is always high in carbon monoxide content and its inhalation is detected by analysing the blood for carboxyhaemoglobin (which is a compound produced in the blood when carbon monoxide combines with the haemoglobin and displaces the oxygen). This compound also produces a cherry red discolouration of the tissues which was quite obvious in both their samples. There was nothing to be found either on naked eye or microscopic examination of the organs to indicate that death was due to any other cause. There was no indication that any of the extensive superficial burns had occurred before death. From the presence of the paint like yellowish material smeared over the left shoulder and spattered over the front of the chest and back of the right hand on the body of Tom Wah Kent, one surmises that the deceased had been recently engaged in painting with his shirt off. There is no evidence from the post mortem examination of the bodies to show that Tom Wah Kent had died sometime, say one or more days, before Tom Ling. The state of preservation of both bodies was identical and the findings are those to indicate that both had died about the same time.

    Taken and sworn to me at St. John's,
    This 19th day of December A.D., 1958.

Appendix K

Pursuant to Section 116 of the Summary Jurisdiction Act, Chapter 117, Revised Statutes of Newfoundland, 1952, into the cause of death of Tom Ling, aged 52, of Botwood, Newfoundland, on November 7, 1958

Enquiry held at Grand Falls and St. John's between December 9th and December 19th, 1958.

Enquiry held before: Magistrates A.E. Cramm and J.P. Mulcahy.

Witnesses examined:

Cst. Bruce Gillingham, R.C.M.P., Grand Falls.
Cst. A.A. Bowen, R.C.M.P., Botwood.
Miss Hearsey Canning, Botwood.
Cst. R.L. Healey, R.C.M.P., Grand Falls.
Harry Chow, Windsor.
Harvey Fong, Botwood.
Edgar Buckley, Botwood.
Cpl. D. Foster, R.C.M.P., Grand Falls.
Cst. L.G. Crowe, R.C.M.P., Grand Falls.
Cpl. H. Taylor, R.C.M.P., Grand Falls.
Inspector A. Argent, R.C.M.P., Corner Brook.
Staff Sergeant Joseph G. Fitzpatrick, R.C.M.P. Corner Brook.
Doctor Hugh Twomey, Botwood.
Bennett J. Elliott, Botwood.

Finding: The evidence in the case of Tom Ling is voluminous and exhaustive. The evidence indicates that Tom Ling and Ken Ling, regarded locally as father and son, lived together but not harmoniously. The older man described the younger man as lazy and crazy and there seems to have been spasmodic disagreements. Tom Ling was an erratic creature and seems to have become depressed just prior to his death. This depression could have resulted from a number of causes.

    1. The alleged interference by Ken Ling with his plans to have a bride come from China.
    2. The recent order issued by the local representative of the Department of health whereby he was forbidden to serve food from the kitchen of his restaurant.
    3. The recent disturbance experienced in his restaurant by a group of sailors.
    4. He was an introvert and made no [recent] effort to mix socially even with people of Chinese origin.
    5. He was easily roused and very irritable. He had previously tried to take his own life.

From the evidence submitted it would appear that Tom Ling was depressed and morose on the night before his death. His moroseness was probably agitated by the entry of the R.C.M.P. to his living quarters. Subsequently events would seem to indicate that he became totally insane and in his maniacal fury he decided that he would not be taken alive. He behaved like a maniac and ultimately a fire of unknown origin broke out in the top story of the restaurant. As a result of this fire and the resultant smoke both Tom Ling and his son known locally as Ken Ling, alias Tom Wah Kent, alias Ken Wah Tom died of asphyxiation about the same time.

Dated at Grand Falls this 7th day of January, A.D., 1959.

(A. E. Cramm) Magistrate.

Appendix L

In a report to L. H. Nicholson, Commissioner of the RCMP in Ottawa, dated December 2, 1958, Superintendent A. W. Parsons Commanding "B" Division made some observations regarding the Newfoundland Constabulary's investigation of the Royal Canadian Mounted Police, in which he states:

> With regard to the additional investigation carried out by District Inspector Harold March of the Newfoundland Constabulary, both the Honourable Attorney General and the Deputy Attorney General, in discussing this case with me, felt that a senior member of the Constabulary should go to Botwood to conduct some independent investigation. In this connection, both Mr. Curtis and Mr. Puddester considered that there might be criticism leveled at members of the Force going to the Chinese Quarters when they did, and also there might be criticism of the fact that this Force was the only investigating agency into the death of one of our members.
>
> I objected to this procedure feeling that our men were justified in carrying out their investigation, particularly inasmuch as any and all attempts by persons well acquainted with the Chinese, to have them either come out or show themselves had been to no avail. Additionally, it was fairly well known that there was very bad feelings between the father and son and it could well have been that either one could have been killed. There had been no real attempt to force open the door of the Chinese living quarters, and while the late Cst. Hoey had

made the remark that the members should force their way in, this action was not agreed to by the member i/c who likely felt that the police party could well talk either Tom Ling or his son into coming out. I therefore fail to see where any criticisms would be justified.

Insofar as a member of the Constabulary going to Botwood to carry out an independent investigation is concerned, I objected to this as I felt that it would be tantamount to criticising our investigative methods and leave a definite suspicion that our members were prepared to "whitewash" the affair even though we had no reason to as I say "whitewash" anything. Both Mr. Curtis and Mr. Puddester were rather adamant that there might be criticism of the Force which was something they did not want to see happen and therefore Inspector March was detailed to proceed to Botwood.

Appendix M

This information brought a terse letter from RCMP Commissioner L. H. Nicholson dated January 22, 1959, to the Attorney General, the Honourable L. R. Curtis.

> Dear Mr. Curtis:
> I refer to the investigation into the unfortunate and untimely death of the late Constable Hoey of this Force and that of two Chinese, occurring at Botwood, Newfoundland on November 7th 1958.
> I have read the reports covering the investigation with considerable interest but I must say I was somewhat concerned over the direction that had been issued from your office for an independent investigation by an officer of the Newfoundland Constabulary. It was mentioned in the reports covering the investigation that this action was considered advisable by yourself and the Deputy Attorney General in the best interests of the Force. While I appreciate such a thought it is difficult for me to erase from my mind the thought that such an independent investigation could have an opposite effect and in all probability would indicate to the public a feeling of mistrust on the part of yourself and the Deputy Attorney General.
> The action of the Fire Marshal in having photographs taken by our photographer and retaining the film to have it developed by another organization appears to be the cause for the feeling which I find difficult to dismiss. As no good reason appears in the reports for such

action on the part of the Fire Marshal, the obvious assumption is mistrust.

I hasten to assure you that to my knowledge in the many years of criminal law enforcement work since this Force came into being, there has never been an occasion when it was found necessary or advisable to have another agency conduct an investigation in respect of any matter of which it was the duty of the Force to investigate. I trust that the action taken in connection with this matter will not leave an effect in the mind of the public that would create an adverse feeling toward the members of this Force in the province of Newfoundland. I am sure this is something you would wish to avoid as much as I do.

Appendix N

Feb. 25, 1959.

The Commissioner,
Royal Canadian Mounted Police
Ottawa.

Dear Mr. Commissioner:
I duly received your letter of the 22nd of January.
You will I am sure appreciate my delay in replying. In the first place you realize, of course, just how busy we have been in this Department since the strike started; then there were certain facts I wanted to get, particularly from the Fire Commissioner, who was out of town when your letter arrived.
First of all let me assure you that there is no real reason why you should be concerned over my action in asking for an independent investigation by an officer of the Newfoundland Constabulary into the unfortunate incident in Botwood. I took the action I did for the sole purpose of being able to vindicate the R.C.M.P. should any criticism be leveled at them as a result of the regrettable death of Constable Hoey and the two chinamen, both of whom it appears were still alive when the members of the R.C.M.P. attacked the restaurant.
As you know, when Newfoundland entered Confederation there was considerable ill-feeling in certain quarters and that feeling has sometimes taken shape in criticism of the R.C.M.P. more often than not in cases

where there is no just cause for such criticism. For a while I was irritated by the antics of certain lawyers and by their treatment of R.C.M.P. witnesses in the Magistrate's Court calling in the Magistrates there and insisting that police witnesses be given protection by the Court and not treated as if they are the accused. I believe that now at last such treatment has stopped but every now and then you hear rumblings of criticism, largely from motorists who seem to resent being stopped by the R.C.M.P. even when the Constable is right and they are wrong. The situation is further aggravated by the fact that the coming of the R.C.M.P. into Newfoundland has created a big change in policing from what we had in Newfoundland before Confederation. In the old days as you know we had local policemen who resided, slept and frequently grew fat in many of our settlements. They had very little to do, but their presence in the community gave a feeling of security and comfort to the people. They were there at any time of the day or night and would frequently walk through the settlement. With the coming of the R.C.M.P. conditions changed. Many areas that used to take comfort in the fact that they had a police constable in their midst, found that instead of that they merely got the somewhat rare sight of a couple of R.C.M.P. Constables speeding through their area in a car not stopping, unless they had been contacted earlier in the day. Then again in the night time when Church and other dances were taking place the local policeman was always on the job. With the coming of the R.C.M.P. police visited these areas only if a disturbance occurred and ten chances to one by the time the R.C.M.P. arrived the trouble was over.

For these and other reasons the R.C.M.P. has not been an outstanding success in Newfoundland, though I must add that as Attorney General I have nothing to complain of in the men that you have sent to us nor in their behaviour and conduct while here.

As soon as I learned that both the chinamen were in

Botwood and alive at the time of the Botwood incident, I feared that some of this resentment, resentment which I feel is quite unfair and unwarranted, might flare up, so, in order that I might have something that I could use in defence of the R.C.M.P. I instructed a high ranking officer of the Newfoundland Constabulary to check on what had happened in Botwood. I felt that from the point of view of the public a report from such an officer and a Newfoundlander, would carry more popular support than a report made to me by a senior officer of the R.C.M.P., since of course it was the R.C.M.P. that might have been under attack. I was worried lest the R.C.M.P. be accused of acting too promptly and ill-advisedly during the wee small hours of the morning and during the hours of darkness they endeavoured to enter the restaurant. It is always easy to be wise after the event, and I think that the officers concerned will agree with me now when I suggest that if they had deferred this entry until the next morning the results would not have been as disastrous as they were. I realize, of course, that feelings were running very high in Botwood, particularly after Constable Hoey's death, but it does seem to me the need for haste was unduly stressed by the woman in the case, a character of no outstanding virtue.

It has at no time been emphasized publicly that both these Chinese were in the building and alive at the time the attack took place and time in this case is on our side. Evidence to this effect has not yet been given publicity, and when it does come out the news story, as a story will be cold. This at least is my hope. You will be glad to hear I know that the report of the Newfoundland Constabulary officer was very satisfactory. It has never been released except when such release is in the interests of the R.C.M.P. I am not looking for trouble; I am trying to anticipate it.

I made enquiries from the Fire Commissioner as to the reason why he brought the film you refer to, in to St. John's to be developed. He tells me that there must be a misunderstanding somewhere in this connection. He says that Inspector Argent suggested that he take the film and have it developed in St. John's, not because he had any lack of confidence in the R.C.M.P. but because this was the more convenient thing to do. The R.C.M.P. who were cooperating with the Fire Commissioner in every conceivable way offered to take some pictures for him. He is not a photographer, and in any event did not have a camera. With their usual courtesy the R.C.M.P. offered to take any pictures that he required, and when the pictures were taken I understand the Inspector himself suggested that it might be more convenient if the Fire Commissioner took the film and had it developed in St. John's. I would point out of course that the Fire Commissioner was investigating the cause of the fire and the pictures he took were only for the purpose of supplementing his report. There was no question whatever at any time of any difference of opinion between the Fire Commissioner and the R.C.M.P.; indeed he commented most favourably on the cooperation that he received.

Finally let me assure you that what I did I did in good faith, feeling that it was in the interest of the R.C.M.P. to do so, and I regret very much that you should put any other interpretation on my action, which as I have said was dictated with the friendliest of motives.

While from your point of view an enquiry by one of your own offices is most satisfactory, I still feel that from the point of view of an outsider, an independent report wold carry much more weight. Were the position reversed tomorrow and were any possibility that the Newfoundland Constabulary might be under fire I would unhesitatingly ask your permission to have one of your officers conduct a similar investigation.

May I in closing express my appreciation of the cooperation that we have received from the R.C.M.P. during the present strike in Newfoundland. I have found Superintendent Parsons and Inspector Argent most cooperative. The reports I hear from the Mainland about their exceeding their authority are absolutely without any justification. In fact, the police could and possibly should have gone even further than they did at any time. For fifty-four days now certain entrance gates owned by the Company have been in the possession of the strikers and still are. The police might well have been instructed to return possession of these gates to the Company, but so far we have hesitated to use them for that purpose.

With all good wishes, I remain,

>
> Yours faithfully,
> Leslie R. Curtis
> Attorney General.

Appendix O

April 7, 1959
The Honourable L.R. Curtis, Q.C.,
Attorney General for the Province,
Of Newfoundland \ House of Assembly,
St. John's Newfoundland.

Dear Mr. Curtis:
Thank you for your letter of February 25 in reply to Commissioner Nicolson's letter to you dated January 22 dealing with the unfortunate incident which occurred in Botwood, Newfoundland, resulting in the death of one of our Constables and that of two Chinese. I was very glad to receive your letter and to note the reasons contained therein for the special investigation called by you to be carried out by the Newfoundland Constabulary.

    I note what you have to say about certain criticisms of our members resulting from the carrying out of their duties. You will appreciate, of course, that a police force cannot hope to operate with any degree of efficiency without criticism of some sort. This applies particularly to traffic cases, as mentioned in your letter.

    It is unfortunate that we encounter cases such as that which occurred in Botwood but I suppose so long as we carry out police duties we are more or less bound to become associated with such unhappy incidents.

Yours sincerely,
C.E. Rivett-Carnac, Commissioner, R.C.M.P.

Appendix P

Articles continue to surface regarding Constable Terry Hoey's shocking death. His life and sacrifice is constantly honoured. Should even a slight diversion from the truth or a blatant error occur, then it is corrected immediately.

Helen Escott, RCMP media relations specialist, wrote the following in a letter to the *Evening Telegram*, December 27, 2002.

> I am responding to the letter from Helen Fogwill Porter titled "Police and Guns. Dec. 19."
>
> In it she says, "In my recollection, the only R.C.M.P. officer shot to death in Newfoundland was killed by his own gun."
>
> I would correct this information, as it is a serious injustice to police officers in this province.
>
> The R.C.M.P. has had two members killed in Newfoundland.
>
> CONSTABLE TERRY HOEY
>
> Cst. Terry Hoey was 21 years old when he was serving in Botwood, Nov. 6, 1958.
>
> Cst. Hoey, along with two other R.C.M.P. members, responded to a domestic dispute between the owner of a local restaurant and his son. After getting no response from inside the living quarters of the restaurant and fearing for the son's life, the three members entered a side window and knocked on the living room door.
>
> They received no answer and found the door had been heavily barricaded. They called out to the owner and asked him to open the door. Immediately, a shotgun

blast ripped through the wood of the closed door, striking Cst. Hoey in the chest. He died at the scene.

A great part of his family's sorrow was in knowing that Terry wanted to be a policeman all his life, and that wish had led him to his death.

CONSTABLE ROBERT AMEY

Cst. Robert Amey was 24 years old when he was killed Dec 17, 1964, in Whitbourne. Four men broke out of Her Majesty's Penitentiary in St. John's. They stole a car and headed west along the Trans-Canada Highway. Near Whitbourne, they ran through a roadblock that had been set up by Csts. David Keith and Robert Amey.

A chase ensued, and the four soon abandoned their car and ran for cover. They were discovered hiding in Whitbourne. Even though they were cornered, they refused to surrender. Amey went to the car radio and called for help. When Amey was in the cruiser the four rushed Cst. Keith and after beating him severely, took away his service revolver.

When Amey came running back, he could see that Keith was down and one of the fugitives was armed. Amey attempted to hold the prisoners at gunpoint but the fugitive fired three shots, one of which hit Amey in the chest, killing him instantly. Using Amey's gun, Cst. Keith was able to arrest all four fugitives.

Besides these two tragic incidents, several R.C.M.P. members have been shot at in this province. Every day I witness one member who limps through our building—he was shot while on patrol. Luckily he lived, but his emotional scars will last forever. His partner was not so lucky—that officer died as a result of his injuries.

I realize that Ms. Fogwill Porter was not aware of the history of this province.

It is an injustice to let Cst. Hoey and Cst. Amey get lost in our history books. These two men gave their lives to protect their communities.

It is that same reality that every police officer in this province faces every time they put on a uniform.

Helen Escott, St. John's

Appendix Q

Report on the contents of cardboard carton accompanying the bodies of "Tom Wah Kent" and "Tom Ling."

> Details:
> A large sealed cardboard carton arrived at the General Hospital, St. John's with the bodies of Tom Wah Kent and Tom Ling on November 8th, 1958. We thought it advisable to hold this carton until someone familiar with the contents was present for the examination who might advise the course of any investigation or analysis that might be required. On November 10th, 1958 at 10:30 the carton was opened in the presence of Corporal Taylor and Const. Bowen of the R.C.M.P. The carton contained a sealed envelope addressed to the Government Pathologist and enclosing a letter which read as follows:
>
> Sir:
>
> This package contains the burnt remnants of a cardboard box in which the body of Tom Wah Kent was lying at the time entry was first made into the burning building.
>   For further particulars please refer to the escorting member Const. F.E.S. Barton.
>
>   Sng: J.G. Fitzpatrick.
>   Staff-Sergeant of Botwood, Nfld.,
>   November 7th, 1958

Examination:
The contents of the box consisted of (1) an irregular slab of water soaked wallboard which was heavily burnt and scorched, (2) burnt and water soaked scraps of wood and of wall board, (3) fragments of glass such as might come from a window pane several of which were partially covered with paint similar in nature to that found on the body of Tom Wah Kent, and with black soot on the pieces, (4) charred debris. None of these revealed any stains such as blood. One piece of painted glass was removed and preserved and the remainder of the contents were turned over to the R.C.M.P. No specific tests or analyses were requested or performed

Ken Ling: What led to his death?

Ken's body was located in the living quarters, face up, and on his back near a wall, lying in a breadbox. He was close to Jim's body, which lay on the chesterfield. His father's body was warm and quivered when he was moved. Ken's was ice cold, contorted, and stiff as a board. This convinced nearly everyone, apart from Dr. Twomey, that he had been dead for some time, and possibly even days. Twomey, ever the professional, elected to await the findings of the provincial pathologist.

Very experienced and intelligent people shared that assessment, and with good reason. Rigor mortis appeared to have locked Ken's body in a rigid state. That belief gave rise to much folklore in the absence of a magisterial enquiry report. It became a question of just how did Jim kill his son, and not whether or not he did. Speculation was varied, running from some "special Chinese martial arts hold," to shooting, poisoning through injection, and stabbing. Moreover, the intended ultimate disposition of Ken's body had numerous possibilities as well, some quite hideous.

The reader will note that the pathologist's report indicated they both died around the same time from similar causes, chiefly carbon monoxide poisoning. How could the state of Ken's body be reconciled with these findings? Surely, dead men don't breathe, except perhaps in movies, yet there was no doubt. Carbon monoxide and soot particles had led to the death of both at approximately the same time. Yet, Ken was found "ice cold and stiff as a board." Perhaps looking deeper is in order.

What if it was not rigor mortis they were viewing but something quite different?

In the 1950s, the science of hypothermia was rather primitive compared to that of today. The word itself usually conjured up images of individuals dying as a result of being immersed in water for a considerable time, or subjected to winter conditions like storms, or caught on the ice floes. Images of people dying in such conditions elicit horrifying thoughts of lost loved ones. But over time it became clear that people can also die from hypothermia under quite different conditions than those described.

When the human body's core temperature falls below 35 degrees Celsius (95°F), hypothermia commences. It can occur when the temperature of a room slowly falls, that is to say it does not require immediate and bitter conditions. During power failures, for example, seniors have died from hypothermia in prolonged cool temperatures, not necessarily at the freezing point. There are three stages: mild, moderate, and severe.

In the *moderate* stage, the individual shivers, which eventually stops as the hypothermia progresses, becomes quite confused, becomes indifferent to his or her condition, exhibits slurred speech or mumbling, shallow breathing, becomes drowsy, and begins to slide toward unconsciousness. The gradual onset of hypothermia often leads to the individual being unaware of what is actually happening.

The *severe* stage advances to present extreme confusion, amnesia, inability or difficulty speaking, the inability to use one's hands, stumbling, stupor, difficulty walking, terminal burrowing, and paradoxical undressing.

Terminal burrowing occurs in the final stages of hyperthermia, prior to death. It is sometimes referred to as "hide and die syndrome." The afflicted seeks small enclosed places like a small room, a wardrobe, or possibly, in this case, a breadbox. It is "hibernating" behaviour caused by anatomic triggering in the brain, not a conscious decision.

This burrowing is sometimes associated with paradoxical undressing, behaviour exhibited by the hypothermic victim now disoriented, confused, and combative. He flails around, discarding his clothing, just the opposite of what he needs to do to stay alive.

Rescue teams often find people trapped in avalanches or snowdrifts displaying similar behaviour. Further, seniors found in unheated homes, especially females, have been incorrectly tagged as having been sexually assaulted when found in a state of nakedness.

> **Harbourview Cafe**
> Conditions inside 11:00 a.m. (approximately)
> November 7th, 1958
> As Per Statement of Dec 11, 1958
> Inspector Arthur Argent, R.C.M.P.
>
> ... I found the building damp and cold, no heat apparently had been in the building for some considerable time [four days]. In the living quarters upstairs, no heating apparatus was to be found. The only heat going to this section of the building being from downstairs.

While applying the above information to allow some speculation, bearing in mind it is just that, speculation, let us revisit Monday's scene as Frank Adams and Edgar Buckley depart, leaving Jim and Ken alone at the café. The Lings are engaged in an intense discussion regarding Ken's wife. Jim is unwell, either because of a cold or the pressure of his litany of problems. Their conversation continues up the stairs and into the living room. Jim is shocked to learn that Ken's wife is not coming.

There Ken makes another revelation. It is the last straw. He shows Jim his packed suitcase and tells him outright that he is leaving, too. He has made arrangements for Tuesday. Ken cannot take it anymore, living away from his wife, and life held too many potential problems for his family. His clothes have been ironed and packed, and he is happy to be leaving and wishes Jim well.

Jim can't believe it. This cannot possibly be, not after all he has done. In spite of their differences, Jim still thinks of Ken as his son and wants to build a life around that, which naturally involves the presence of Ken's wife. As cruel as it was, he has accepted the fact that his own bride is not coming because of Ken's letter. His mind goes to his discussions with Hearsey and the news that she is leaving the café and going to Norway. Hearsey, his "Boey," who has been such a friend to both himself and Ken. There is an upcoming court date regarding the damaged German boy, and the café is still without a food licence. Moreover, the Germans are coming to kill them both.

And now, his son is telling him he is leaving. That will take him back to where he was in 1931, alone and playing cards with men, without a family life, and the lifestyle as prescribed by Confucius is now absolutely and forever out of reach. No, Ken cannot go, he must not go! Life will be meaningless without him! I will not let him go!

Jim takes his .22-calibre rifle and orders Ken into Jim's room and barricades the door with the chesterfield. He will keep him here, even if it is against his will. Jim Ling has crossed the line.

The stove downstairs, the only stove currently in the building operational, is lit, but Jim is so exhausted he lies down on the chesterfield chair and falls asleep. Ken, now barred in the windowless bedroom, soon falls asleep on Jim's bed. The fire goes out. It is 40°F outside and will remain so for four days. A brief lighting of the downstairs stove will occur only twice during this period, each time triggering futile attempts on the part of Hearsey and others to establish contact. Meanwhile, Ken is in the midst of creeping hypothermia. Wearing two sweatshirts, he is not dressed for the cold, and there is only a set of bedsheets on the bed. In a matter of hours, the blood flow to his limbs and skin decreases and pools in his core organs in an attempt to keep him alive. He is afraid Jim may shoot him if he cries out for help. And will anyone hear him anyway, as he is contained in the bedroom without windows?

It is Wednesday. His shivering stops. He tries to call out but realizes he is unable to speak. He tries to stand but cannot. He is in a state of confused euphoria, unaware of the danger he is in.

It is now Thursday night and his body's core temperature is at 86°F and he is sleepy. He is unaware that Hearsey is outside, standing on a bank, calling out. His brain is on autopilot now, and he seeks a place to curl up, to burrow. The two shirts he is wearing are simply of no use, and in the room he fixates on a cardboard box on the floor. It's been there all along, nothing unusual there.

His brain now directs him to use that confined space for burrowing and as a source of heat. Ken doesn't realize it, but cardboard is a good heat conductor.

With effort, he rolls off the mattress and bedspring right into the breadbox, making a lot of noise, ending in a loud bang. The noise is heard outside. Startled, Jim, dressed more warmly, who had been outside the door pacing around and swinging his arms to stay warm, pushes the chesterfield blocking the door aside and opens the bedroom door. He drags Ken, who is immobilized and still in the breadbox, out into the living area. He leaves him there, on his back and face up, his arms contorted. Ken is totally unable to move now, and as the hours drag slowly by, he drifts toward unconsciousness.

Again a confused and mentally deranged Jim Ling sits down in the chesterfield chair holding the rifle. Ken's core temperature continues to drop overnight, and unbeknownst to him, the process of paradoxical undressing kicks in, leaving him partially naked. He is nearing death as his core temperature now gradually drops even further, to 81°F. His extremities are ice cold. He lies immobile now in a total state of unconsciousness, but still breathing, though very shallowly. He was indeed partially naked.

Outside, the town has gone frantic. It is 8:30 a.m. and police cars are everywhere Out of nowhere a tear-gas canister flies into the room, followed quickly by another, and the room explodes into flames and tear gas. Near death from hypothermia, Ken struggles to breathe. Guns are being fired. He manages to draw several breaths. Sadly, Ken's life ends. He will die from carbon monoxide poisoning, as will his father. Within an hour, people enter the room and find him cold and stiff as a board. Understandably, they conclude he has been dead for some considerable time, the symptoms being similar to rigor mortis. Could this have happened? The author thinks so. Perhaps the reader can speculate as to whether or not there is another possibility.

Appendix R

Yvonne Chow

In 1956, Mrs. Chow came to Newfoundland to join her husband, Tom, at the Taiwan Restaurant in Grand Falls. Following the incident, she wrote a letter to Hong Seto, her husband's mother, who was resident in Hong Kong at that time. Hong Seto then told Ah Yee about the tragedy, and also Ah Yee's mother, who was her second cousin.

Ah Yee then came to St. John's, Newfoundland, in the early 1960s with her young son, Don Tom, and rented a bed-sitting room over Tom's Takeout on Gower Street. Once the estate matters had been resolved, Ah Yee, at the insistence of Hong Seto, who had relocated to Grand Falls in 1959, moved to Grand Falls to live and work at the Taiwan Restaurant with the Chows. There Ah Yee remained for several years, where Don Tom and May Soo, the Chows' young daughter, went to Notre Dame Academy. Eventually Ah Yee moved to Toronto, where in 2000 she passed away at the age of seventy. Don Tom continues to live in Ontario with his son.

Interview: William Ping

"Dad, William Ping, Sr., owned the Snow White Laundry, the last Chinese laundry in St. John's, and was instrumental in having a memorial to the Chinese placed on the site where it once stood immediately across from City Hall. Ping was the subject of a film called *The Last Chinese Laundry*, which told of the struggles of immigrants in his time. It can be viewed on You-

Tube. He was also the person assigned the task of painting Chinese lettering on all headstones in St. John's, and it is his work that can be seen on the photograph of the headstone of Tom and Ken Ling."

Jean Fong Jine

With tear-filled eyes, Jean Fong Jine recalls when she and her mother were going through immigration. They were taken to separate rooms and interviewed independently. Neither spoke English at the time, and Jean was just fifteen. They were asked, "How many chickens do you have? How many chickens do your neighbours have? What are the names of your neighbours and the names of their children, and how old are they?"

It was brutal, but somehow they got through it.

"We were treated like criminals, criminals. When Dad [Harvey Fong] and Charlie met us at the station on our arrival, they were both crying, because they understood what we had been put through." Jean stops to compose herself as she relives the trauma of the experience. "Dad had not seen me before, nor Winnie for fifteen years. Our reunion was a dream come true." Any loneliness Harvey felt quickly faded, and Jean was to be joined by six siblings in rather short order. She proudly displays the letter of apology from the prime minister and relates how proud her mother, Winnie, was to receive it and compensation for the "head tax."

Jean points out, "The Chinese Community did not abandon Jim. I believe that when he shot the cop he went out of his mind. There was no turning back."

Interview: Dave Fong

"William Fong, my father, came to Newfoundland in 1928, twenty-one years before the communist revolution. He was from Can Tong, in southern China near Hong Kong, which has a population four times that of Canada. He came in search of an opportunity for riches and wages that far exceeded what was being earned in China.

"In Botwood he met and married Shirley Richardson, a Caucasian lady, and they opened and operated a successful magazine and confectionary store. Like most Chinese, he spoke seldom of home, where conditions were so bleak that villages got together to sponsor for emigration a person most likely to succeed. William knew Jim and did socialize with him, but Jim's expectations far exceeded what the relationship could provide. Unlike the majority of Chinese, he chose to be buried in Botwood upon his passing."

Shirley Fong

Shirley Fong, widow of William Fong, spoke of the tough struggle her Chinese husband, William, had when he came over to Newfoundland. Her husband had been made whole, her family's dignity brought into the sunlight. Mrs. Fong was proud to show the author the apology letter she received from the Canadian government for past wrongs to her departed Chinese husband. She, too, received the remuneration that went to survivors of the brutal head tax the Chinese had to endure.

Interview: Carol Ann Thompson Godo

"Our whole family were great friends with Red Bowen. Dad and Mom took us all up to Grand Falls shopping two days before all this happened, and Terry met up with Artie Daye at Bowring's. They each bought identical watches, and Terry, having tried on his, said, 'I won't be needing the case,' and gave Dad the watch case. It's still in the family, in light of what happened.

"The day after the incident, Red came in the house, sat at the table, and poured out the entire story in great detail. Never had we seen anyone so consumed in loss and sorrow. His words were interrupted with loud sobbing and pauses. We all cried along with him that day. It was a coming together of broken people lost in grief for the loss of a beautiful Mountie and close friends. Dad and Jim were very close. I will never forget it, ever.

"You know what is odd? That event did not stop the interaction with the Chinese residents whatsoever. Wong feared there may be some repercussions and closed his store for a couple of days. There were none, and he soon reopened. There were no racial overtones at all.

"We, as a community, were all beaten down by the event and struggled to understand it. We waited and waited for the magisterial report to be released, and it never was."

Interview: Linda Canning Brovig, niece to Hearsey Canning

"I'll never forget that night.

"It was cold enough to clip you, with misty rain and snow flurries. Jim went berserk that night. He was afraid that Ken was going to leave him. . . . He was afraid that Hearsey was going to leave him, too, and go to Norway. In spite of it all, Jim still thought of Ken as a son. He just wanted him to stay, that's all, whether Ken wanted to or not. Otherwise, Jim's life was gone, everything he lived for. He was holding on to his life and dreams the best way he could. And he didn't mean to kill the young Mountie, either. He just wanted everything to be peaceful and for people to 'go away.' How many times did he say that? It was so sad. Jim was no monster. He was a very kind man, but rough around the edges, who had much love to give away and no one to give it to."

Arising out of the magisterial enquiry, interesting enough are some items, assuming, of course, its purpose was to get to the truth, from which findings can be rendered, and possible recommendations made to facilitate a more appropriate approach to future responses, wherein deaths and injuries can be avoided altogether or at least minimized. One would not want to have the public perceive a "whitewashing," as referenced by the RCMP commissioner in his letter to the Attorney General.

In his thorough letter forwarded to the Officer Commanding on November 20, 1958, Inspector Argent points out that, regarding the upcoming enquiry, "all witnesses with the exception of Mr. LeDrew now hospitalized at St. John's are available." One might conclude that means all witnesses the RCMP had interviewed were ready, presumably to substantiate their statements and have their knowledge examined on the stand, hence getting to the facts in the case.

If that be the case, then one can only speculate as to why the following were not called: Don Boone; Warrick Swyers; Gordon Locke; Frank Adams; and Linda Canning. These individuals were right in the midst of the drama. Why were Lang Nichols, Bill Butler, nor Hugo Thulgreen asked by either the RCMP or the Newfoundland Constabulary or the enquiry for a statement? Nichols and Boone had both been present when Hearsey warned both Mounties about Jim Ling's gun. She made this fact known a second time when Nichols was ordered off the ladder by Bowen, at which time she supported Bowen's command by stating, "No, don't let him go in there. Jim has a gun in the building." Especially curious is the testimony of both officers pertaining to having knowledge of the presence of guns in statements given to RCMP and Constabulary and also to the magistrate, in their final sentences on two of their statements: Bowen's enquiry statement concludes with, "I have not been told and I did not know that there were firearms in the café." The Newfoundland Constabulary statement of November 12, 1958, concludes, "I took charge of the guns outside and locked them up." No reference to foreknowledge of guns. The RCMP statement of November 11, 1958, concludes, "At no time did any person tell me the Chinaman had a gun in the café."

And what about Bill Butler, who assisted in carrying Hoey's body from the landing, and raced to get guns from hunters to distribute to unarmed police? He was a long-time friend of Jim Ling. The same could be asked about Fred Gill, Hugo Thulgreen, and Alec Nichols. They had remarkable long-term relationships with the deceased Jim Ling and could have offered much insight and suggestions.

Constable Healey's enquiry statement concludes with, "From the time I was first advised of the situation, when I met Constables Bowen and Hoey at Bishop's Falls, I had not been told and I had no reason to believe that either of the occupants of the Harbourview Cafe was armed." His Constabulary statement of November 11 concludes, "I stayed there until replacements came. Constable Hoey died shortly after being shot. Dr.

Twomey pronounced him dead." No reference to knowledge of guns. His RCMP statement of November 11, as an amendment, concludes, "Further to the above statement. I wish to state that at no time was I informed that either of the Chinese had a gun in the building."

Hearsey Canning's enquiry statement comes to an abrupt end when she states, "Two policemen arrived in a motor car, and I told them that Tom Ling had locked himself in his café and that he might have done some harm to Jim." Her RCMP statement of November 10, 1958, states, "I told the Mounties that Mr. Ling had a gun in his quarters. We went around to the kitchen window." Her Newfoundland Constabulary statement of November 12, 1958: "Constable Bowen asked me if the Chinaman had a gun before they picked up the man in civilian clothes. I mentioned to the officers that I believed Jim had hurt Ken so the latter could not talk."

Did she not have more to add to her enquiry statement? Was she not the one who had tried to the point of exhaustion, commencing on Tuesday through Thursday inclusive, to have someone in authority engage the police? Did she not put her own life in danger on the roof of the porch where she heard the gun cock, and on the ladder in a failed attempt to dialogue with Jim to ascertain the whereabouts of Ken, whom many, including herself, believed may have been injured or killed by his father? To not have informed the officers regarding the fact that she knew there was a gun on the property is beyond belief. To not have done so would be tantamount to an admission of negligence on her part and that of Harry Chow and Harvey Fong. Further, the weight of the guilt of such an oversight and any ensuing abuse wrongly cast her way would be an almost impossible load to bear. Nothing is being implied here. It is merely perusal of stated and signed statements.

What does Linda have to say?

Sworn Statement of Linda Canning, November 10, 1958

My name is Linda Canning. I am fifteen years of age. My date of birth is. . . . I live at Botwood with my mother, Mrs. Ada Canning, and my aunt Hearsey Canning. She used to work at the Harbourview Cafe in Botwood. A Chinaman named Jim Ling owned the café.

On Thursday afternoon about 4:00 I went with my aunt Hearsey to the Spot Cash store in Botwood. This store is owned by another Chinaman. My aunt wanted to talk to this man, because Jim Ling had not opened his café since Monday, the third of November, and she was afraid that there was trouble with him. The Chinaman told my aunt to go down to the Harbourview Cafe and try to get in herself. This Chinaman at the Spot Cash would not go along with us. He told us that if we couldn't get in Jim's place to telephone him back. We came to the Harbourview Cafe and found both front doors and the only rear door locked or barred from the inside. It was about 4:30 p.m. now, and we started tapping with our hands on the windows and calling out to Jim Ling to come out, and asking him if he was in and that she wanted to speak with him. She knocked on all the doors, repeating the same thing, but got no answer. We left the vicinity of the Harbourview Cafe and then walked to a store owned by Mr. Frank Adams near the Botwood Stores on the rear of Water Street. Aunt Hearsey asked Mr. Adams if he would accompany her later in the evening to the Harbourview Cafe, so she could again call out to Jim Ling and ask him that she wanted him. She went to Mr. Adams's because she knew that Jim Ling and Mr. Adams were good friends. We left Mr. Adams's store and walked to our home on Northern Arm Road. It was now about 5:15 p.m. We had our supper. After supper, Aunt Hearsey and myself dressed ourselves and walked to Mr. Frank Adams's house, shortly after 7:00 p.m. We waited for Mr. Adams to dress himself, and then he accompanied us to Jim Ling's café. I noticed that the building was completely blacked out, with the exception of a light showing through a window of a room on the rear of the building upstairs. My aunt told me that the light was shining from the room occupied by Jim Ling was his bedroom. I noticed that this room had three windows and that the blinds were drawn completely down, covering two windows, and the third window was almost completely covered by a blind. It was through this partly uncovered window that I saw the light. This building that I am talking about is a two-storey structure. The window that I saw the light coming through is upstairs to the rear of the building.

The three of us walked around the Harbourview Cafe to the rear of the building, and we put a ladder up to the roof of a new section that had just recently been constructed. The roof of this new section is joined to the building directly under the windowsills of the window I have referred to. My aunt climbed the ladder and got out on this roof and tapped against both windows with her hands. There was no answer. She called out, "Jim, Jim, is something the matter?" There was no answer. We walked over to the east side of the building. There is a partly constructed chimney there, the top of which is close to the ground, and my aunt cupped her hands and sang out again to Mr. Ling. There was no answer. We walked to Mr. Adams's house then again and telephoned the Chinaman at the Spot Cash and asked if he could suggest anything for us to do. He told us to telephone the Mounties if we like. Aunt Hearsey and I waited awhile, and we walked down to the RCMP office in Botwood. There we waited until the RCMP came, and we walked out to the police car in which they were sitting, and Aunt Hearsey told Constable Bowen and another young RCMP whom he called Terry that a young Chinaman who lived at the Harbourview Cafe with Jim Ling was missing. This young Chinaman was known locally as Ken. We both got in the RCMP car with the police and drove up to the Harbourview Cafe. The four of us got out of the police car and walked around the café building. The light was still on in the same room upstairs. It was now around 10:00 p.m. Constable Bowen climbed the ladder to the roof of the newly constructed section on the rear of the Harbourview Cafe and went and tapped on both windows and called out to Jim Ling. I did not hear any reply. Constable Bowen called out, "Jim, come out, is Ken in there with you?" There was still no reply. He got down then to the ground by way of the ladder and told Terry to bring the ladder around to the east side. Constable Terry brought it along and put it up to the window that Aunt Hearsey said could be opened from the outside. The ladder was put up to this window and Constable Bowen climbed up to it. He opened it and called out saying, "Jim, Jim, this is Constable Bowen, the fellow you call Red. I am the policeman who comes to help you when you are in trouble, come out, there is nobody going to hurt you." There was no answer. Constable Bowen stepped halfway down the ladder and Aunt Hearsey told him that Jim Ling had a gun in the building. Constable Bowen then got completely down, and Aunt Hearsey climbed the ladder and put her head in through the window and called out saying, "Jim, Jim, this is Hearsey—Boey." He used to call her Boey. "Come down, we want you." Jim Ling answered saying, "No, no, me don't know you." She got down off the ladder then. A man named Lang Nichols came along then, and he climbed the ladder and called out to Jim. There was no reply at all. Constable Bowen said, "You're not going in there, Lang." And Aunt Hearsey said, "No, don't let him go in, as Jim got a gun in there." Lang Nichols got down off the ladder and Constable Bowen got up the ladder again and closed the window almost completely shut. Constable Bowen got down then and said that he couldn't go in the café unless he had a warrant. He said to Aunt Hearsey, "What are we going to Grand Falls to get a warrant for?" Aunt Hearsey said, "Because there is a Chinaman missing." So then Constable Bowen and the other RCMP man they called "Terry" left and went toward Grand Falls. Aunt Hearsey and I went into Mr. Adams's then because Constable Bowen told her to have an eye on the building and to not let anyone else sing out to Jim. We, that is Aunt Hearsey and myself, went into Frank Adams's house and waited until the RCMP constables got back. When they came back, about 11:45 p.m., there was another member of the RCMP with them. The third RCMP man got up on the ladder and hoisted the same window up in the east side of the building and called out to Jim Ling. He called out, "Jim, Jim, come down, we want you." I did not hear a reply. This new RCMP man got in through the window, and Constable Bowen said, "If he goes in, I go in, too," and he pulled off his coat and gave it to Aunt Hearsey. Terry said, "I am going in, too." He took off his coat and gave it to me. And then Constable Bowen said to Aunt Hearsey, "You go up and watch the back window." Aunt Hearsey walked out to the rear window, and then she walked back again, and then we heard a gunshot. One of the RCMP men said, "He's shot. Call a doctor." Aunt Hearsey and I let out a squeal and went to Mr.

Adams's house and asked him to phone for a doctor, as there was someone shot.

Aunt Hearsey thought that it was Jim Ling who was shot. Someone came to Mr. Adams's door then and asked her if she would go and turn on the lights in the Harbourview Cafe downstairs. Aunt Hearsey went down. Later on, Aunt Hearsey came back crying. She said that it was Terry, the little Mountie, that had been shot. It was shortly after midnight.

That is all I know. I stayed around the area with a group of other people until 4:00 a.m.

>   Witness: Cpl. D.G. Foster
>   Sgd. Linda Canning
>   R.C.M.P.

Appendix S

November Seven
by Fred Budgell

Now come hear my story, it's sad but it's true
Of shooting and dying, In Cafe Harbourview
On November 7, five past twelve o'clock
Jim Ling killed a Mountie, with Number 12 shot

On our way back from Windsor, Fred, Ted, Russ, and Mac
Drove down into Botwood, and nearing the track
Saw that street lights were off, yet floodlights were on
And a Mountie was standing there, holding a gun

We drove up beside him and he told us the score
How a young rookie Mountie had been shot through the door
Me and Ted slipped inside though 'twas late in the night
Would he once more start shooting? We were frozen with fright

There were townspeople everywhere milling about
Afraid we'd be hit, and we wouldn't get out
That night we all waited, with the rain falling fast
And at eight in the morning they brought in tear gas

Through a rear upstairs window, the gas was shot in
And inside their quarters, flames killed Ken and Jim
Their lives had turned hopeless, those men of strange ways
Both dead, their hearts broken, what more can I say

FRED HUMBER

> Three people cut down, we hope they're in heaven
> Botwood's worst nightmare, was November Seven.
>
> *In memory of J. Terrance Hoey, RCMP,*
> *Citizens Jim Ling and Wah Kent Tom, father and son.*
>
> *All died November 7, 1958.*

Acknowledgements

Thanks to the following who through interviews, pictures, and/or information have made this offering possible. Forgive me if someone was overlooked. Everyone's help is appreciated.

Special thanks is extended to May Soo and her mother, Yvonne Chow, who provided extraordinary support when they learned of this book project. They allowed me access to very personal information, files, and pictures of family members, and introduced me to others who provided insight into the Chinese culture and life among immigrants.

Thanks to Garry Cranford, who, by way of a chance meeting in Grand Falls, encouraged me to take on this project, having heard an abbreviated overview of this extraordinary event. He introduced me later to the Flanker Press crew, including his wife, Margo, and son Jerry, and their very talented team. Thanks also to Donna Morrissey, whose editing abilities put me on track to tell the story. She dared to have the gall to kick me out of my own book, and I'm glad she did.

Special thanks to: The Rooms Archive; Centre for Newfoundland Studies; Janette Boone Cooper; Ruth Boone; Botwood Heritage Society; John Brayley; Fred Budgell; Pattie Budgell; Bill and Dorothy Butler; Dennis Butt; Dennis Byrne; Marie Byrne Watkins; Carolyn Atkinson, CBC; Linda Canning Brovig; Juanita Thomson Chayter; Yvonne Chow; Artie Daye; Ralph DeGroot; Eric Edison; Malvina Elliott; Janet Evans Young; Dave, Robert, Linda, and Shirley Fong; Reese Getson; Fred Gill; Merium Duff Gill; Carol Anne Thompson Godo; Patricia Hoey Fryer; John Horwood; Harvey Hue; Dr. Robert E. Humber; Nelson and Doreen Jewer; Jean Fong and Johnny Jine; Hank

FRED HUMBER

Johnston; Hedley and Reg LeDrew; Ken Maher; Gerald Mews; Ted Mills; NL Courts Archive; Dave Nichols; Judy Noseworthy; Doug Pack; Dorm Parsons; Kim Hammond, Peterborough Archives; William Ping; RCMP in Newfoundland and Labrador and Ottawa; Florence Regular; Sylvia Rice; Paddy Ryan; Robert Sandursky; Junior and Desmond Simon; Hilda Snow; May Soo; Warrick Swyers; Hugo Thulgreen; Gloria Young; Roy Young; Joan Warman; Elmo Waterman; Ken and Marie Wells; Jerry "Jed" Woolridge; and Bob Woolridge.

And one more. An extra special thanks to my wife, Yvonne.

Sources

Botwood Heritage Society. *Botwood: History of a Seaport.* Grand Falls–Windsor: Print Atlantic, 1992.
Lahey, Gerald. *The Mounties.* St. John's: Creative Book Publishing, 2004.
Ricketts, J. A. *The Badger Riot.* St. John's: Flanker Press, 2010.
Pitts, Frank. *Confessions of a Mountie.* St. John's: Flanker Press, 2016.

Online Research

Road to Justice: Chinese Exclusion Act. www.roadtojustice.ca/laws/chinese-exclusion-act
History of Chinese immigration to Canada. Wikipedia
Paper sons. Wikipedia
"Chinese Marriage Through a Foreigner's Eyes" by Alan Paul Trundley. https://www.travelchinaguide.com/intro/social_customs/marriage/customs.htm
Ancient Chinese Marriage Customs. https://www.chinahighlights.com/travelguide/culture/ancient-chinese-marriage-customs.htm
"Paper Sons," Hidden pasts. http://articles.latimes.com/2009/aug/02/opinion/oe-see2
Taking Root Exhibit—Chinese Immigration.
Harper Apologizes for Head Tax. https://www.theglobeandmail.com/news/national/pm-offers-apology-symbolic-payments-for-chinese-head-tax/article711245/
Newfoundland and Labrador Apologizes for Head Tax. http://www.cbc.ca/news/canada/newfoundland-labrador/n-l-

apologizes-for-chinese-head-tax-1.614006
Chinese Communist Revolution. Wikipedia.
Chinese Pigtail History. Wikipedia.
Sacrificing for a Better Life.
Monument Marks Head Tax History. http://www.cbc.ca/news/canada/newfoundland-labrador/monument-marks-chinese-head-tax-history-1.942159
The Chiniese in Newfoundland, 1895–1949. http://www.nlhro.org/D78/history
Mu Li Wanderers Between Cultures: Exploring the Individual Expressions of Chineseness in Newfoundland 2014. http://research.library.mun.ca/8192/

Constable John Terrance Hoey, RCMP.
RCMP Constable Terry Hoey Memorial.
Celebrating 60 Years in Newfoundland and Labrador.
About the RCMP in Newfoundland and Labrador.
Honoured in Places - Remembered Mounties across Canada.
Not Forgotten - News - *Advertiser*.
Botwood - The War Years.
Hypothermia - The Mayo Clinic.
Paul Kirtlip's Blog - Hypothermia.
Hypothermia. Wikipedia.
Hypothermia - How to avoid it.
Health Link BC - Cold Temperature Exposure.
The Study of Loneliness - The Mitt Press - Frieda Fromm Reichmann.

Frederick Gerald Humber was born in Botwood, Newfoundland and Labrador, on October 26, 1945. Following high school, he tried numerous entry-level jobs, and in 1963, like many thousands of other Newfoundlanders, he went to Toronto, returning home the following year. The culture shock of city life was not for him. Fortunately, fate would have him cross paths with several other aspiring young musicians, which provided a dream-fulfilling opportunity to play in a professional band travelling the province. From there he attended Mount Allison University as well as Memorial University. Upon graduation in 1973, he entered the field of corrections and child welfare. In 1978, he joined a large life insurance company, where he worked until retirement.

On the evening of November 6, 1958, while taking his first guitar lesson on Burt's Lane in Botwood, an unusual and frightening event took place. It affected Fred Humber so dramatically, it stayed with him over the years. A number of chance encounters in 2013 led him to make the decision to get to the bottom of the great tragedy that rocked his hometown, the province, and the country. Three lives had been lost, two citizens wounded, and a business owned by a long-time Chinese citizen destroyed. Rumours abounded. An enquiry was held but was never released. Long-term suffering was visited upon first responders and the townspeople that lasted for over fifty-eight years. Many people went to their graves never knowing the facts.

Death at the Harbourview Cafe is Fred Humber's first book. It was conceived and researched to finally give relief to those who are left and to enlighten our youth about this historic event, which had almost been forgotten, often becoming confused with two other tragic events, in Badger and Whitbourne. Just what were the answers to the many lingering questions? The mission was to find the truth: not to assign blame, but to restore the event to its rightful place in the history of both Newfoundland and Labrador and the RCMP.